Trined in
Twilight

Books by Mary Summer Rain

Nonfiction
Spirit Song
Phoenix Rising
Dreamwalker
Phantoms Afoot
Earthway
Daybreak
Soul Sounds
Whispered Wisdom
Ancient Echoes
Bittersweet
Mary Summer Rain On Dreams
The Visitation
Millennium Memories
Fireside
Eclipse
The Singing Web
Beyond Earthway
Trined In Twilight

Children's
Mountains, Meadows and Moonbeams
Star Babies

Fiction
The Seventh Mesa

Audio Books
Spirit Song
Phoenix Rising
Dreamwalker
Phantoms Afoot
The Visitation

Trined in Twilight

Mary Summer Rain

HAMPTON ROADS
PUBLISHING COMPANY, INC.

for the evolving human spirit

Cover concept by Mary Summer Rain
Cover design by Marjoram Productions
Cover art "Twilight's Door" copyright © 2000 by Sally

For information write:

Hampton Roads Publishing Company, Inc.
1125 Stoney Ridge Road
Charlottesville, VA 22902

Or call: 804-296-2772
FAX: 804-296-5096
e-mail: hrpc@hrpub.com
Web site: www.hrpub.com

If you are unable to order this book from your local
bookseller, you may order directly from the publisher.
Quantity discounts for organizations are available.
Call 1-800-766-8009, toll-free.

Library of Congress Catalog Card Number: 00-102576
ISBN 1-57174-197-6

10 9 8 7 6 5 4 3 2 1

Printed on acid-free paper in the United States

Dedication

For the Child and Crone
within every woman.

For Little Self, who bravely
shouldered all my childhood grief,
and for the Crone who is so gently
and gracefully coming into her own.

In sweet memory of Shirley M. Miller

Unbeknownst to her, her earthly passion for meticulously repairing antique dolls had only been the beginning of a far greater use of her talents. For now, with loving care, she devotes all her time repairing damaged angel wings.

"I assert that the cosmic religious experience is the strongest and noblest driving force behind scientific research."

"The most beautiful experience we can have is the mysterious . . . the fundamental emotion which stands at the cradle of true art and true science."

— Albert Einstein

"Consciousness is a fascinating phenomenon; it is impossible to specify what it is, what it does or why it evolved."

— Stuart Sutherland, psychologist

"The attainment of Arahatship (The Knowing of Consciousness) will bestow the ecstasy of contemplation, will make (a person) being one to become multiple, being multiple to become one; give the power to call to mind (one's) various temporary states (of being) in days gone by."

— Siddhartha Guatama, Buddha

"Many scientists, from both physical and biological backgrounds, have tackled the question of consciousness."

". . . another group (of scientists) believe that although consciousness is generated by the brain, it is such a special property that it currently defies scientific understanding."

— Susan A. Greenfield, neuroscientist

THE LEGEND

The ancient **Virgin/Mother/Crone** legend attributes the three aspects of the feminine consciousness to a simultaneous indwelling within one's *current* sphere of awareness.

Child/Virgin   Purity. Innocence. Esoteric.
Consciousness remains cognizant and openly receptive to multiple dimensional frequencies of quantum reality.
Of the Spirit.

Mother   Nurturing. Guiding. Knowledge.
Consciousness learns and expands personal spiritual growth through earthly experiential events and intellectual pursuits.
Of the Physical.

Crone   Wisdom. Serenity. Attainment.
Consciousness, full of The Knowing, watches and observes with heightened awareness and understanding.
Of the Mind.

Foreword

Consciousness. An enigma. An enigma because no scientist has been able to give it definitive bounds within which to confine its shape. It has no definition, no molded form, nor limits to its potentiality.

The phenomenology of consciousness remains a continuing bafflement to neuroscientists, because they cannot move away from their idealized penchant to freeze-frame it within the basic physiology of a mechanized physical brain. Therefore they fragment off a minuscule piece of its shimmering totality by reducing it to an encapsulated entity of either the "awareness" state of being conscious, or the "unawareness" condition of unconsciousness, whereby they create and exacerbate their own problematical state of affairs and perpetuate their current conundrum. This firmly imprisons their thought process and prevents a true discovery that would ensue quite naturally through the use of expansive thought. Would they but take it one bold step further, as their physicist counterparts have, they would discover that consciousness requires no gray matter housing to attribute its existence to. The Nobel laureate physicists have dissolved their own former quantum paradoxes by the breakthrough realization that all life is interconnected through a *consciousness* of matter.

This consciousness is the Great Web of Life. Philosophers throughout the ages have given this phenomenology various descriptive terms such as Universal Consciousness, Cosmic Consciousness, Universal Mind, etc. And though we are all firmly connected to this great living consciousness, we also have our own unique consciousness . . . that of individual and personal spirit. Our spirit mind needs no touchable brain matter to function within. Its consciousness is pure thought.

The extent of our consciousness' potential has never been charted, yet we've been allowed glimpses of a few of its incredible talents. Retrogression. Precognition. Remote viewing. Virtual meditation. Yet these only scratch the surface and it's a very weak scratch at that.

Throughout my years of research and study, I've endeavored to vanquish the boundaries of my own knowledge base and understanding by reaching further and further into the Unknowns That Can Be Knowns. Like a pond ripple that widens outward to form a larger and larger ring, my reading has led to the interconnected subjects encompassing ancient and traditional religious beliefs, physics, philosophy, science, metaphysics, anthropology, archaeology, the unearthed Gnostic Gospel Scriptures of the Dead Sea Scrolls, and those from the Nag Hammadi site. Running throughout these interrelated fields of information, certain golden threads wove their ambling way to form a glistening trail that intersected my own experiential path. I found it more than interesting that the physicists' theories regarding Time (that all time could be concurrent or loop over on itself) connected with a legend that intermittently reappeared in ancient texts of various cultures throughout world history. Yet my experiences associated with Time and this Legend took the phenomenon one step further by also proving out that Time was vertical and that my consciousness was poised at the conjunction of vertical and linear time when certain experiences of consciousness were occurring.

So often we hear talk of the Child Within us, yet what of the Elder Within? Since our consciousness has the natural ability to view the future, it would be logical for it to also perceive oneself as an aged individual in her/his later lifetime. For many years now there have been times when I looked in the mirror and had the clear and distinct impression that someone much older was being reflected in the glass; a fleeting sensation, yet solid all the same. And, whenever this happened, the word Crone would come to mind. Throughout these years I'd also experience frequent moments of clear illumination, when brilliant epiphanies of thought or inspired fragments of deep wisdom would suddenly become known to me and I'd rush to finish the intended concept on my own by grabbing my pen and immediately writing down the whole of the concept that initially came to me as a nebulous idea, one that I quickly had to grasp and record before it fled. Oftentimes these would be firm predictions, or they'd come as strong, vivid visuals that I could not brush off as active imaginings. These jewels of enlightenment never had the expressed feel of being generated from an outside intelligence such as the Advisors, a guardian angel, or anyone other than myself as an older, wiser aspect of that current self . . . the Elder Within.

The concept of the Child Within has been a euphemism within multicultural societies since ancient times and, for me personally, was a subtle, living reality that gently and subliminally evinced itself through my life-long interest in collecting children's books that I was particularly drawn to, or as a small child had fond memories of reading. To the right of my small bedroom dormer window is the "child's corner" of my room, where a Raggedy Ann doll sits nestled beside two Teddy bears, and an antique doll is in a rocker in front of the bookcase filled with all the favored childhood books.

Also, beginning in 1990, I began to inexplicably write down a few entries in the two ongoing manuscripts of the companion volumes of my last book set, *Pinecones and Woodsmoke*, regarding a "silver-haired girl child" whom I had the knowing as being the younger aspect of myself . . . of my own present-day consciousness. I'd automatically call her "silver-haired" because she was the child within my consciousness that was now housed within my head of increasingly silver hair. I had the silver hair and she was the child aspect beneath it. Without any literary planning of any kind, entries about this Child and the Crone appeared sporadically among the other thoughts and sayings I'd written in these two working manuscripts. During those times I always thought it was interesting and didn't give it more in-depth consideration than that.

Then, in the fall of 1995, the subtleness of this concept exploded full force into the present when my six-year-old Child Within broke her long-held silence, when she came to the fore of my consciousness and actually spoke to a friend of mine. My Child Within said her name was Little Self and, according to my friend, she acted as precocious as all get-out, while she also evinced her close association with, and thorough knowledge of, the spiritual realm by very matter-of-factly voicing certain predictive revelations about the future and detailing the many historical past-life relationships that my friend and I had shared together.

Little Self was full of exuberance combined with an innocent impishness and an underlying quality of deep wisdom that was far beyond her six-year-old age. She clearly maintained a dimensional positioning that straddled the spiritual and physical realms of reality. She manifested three times that fall and has since been silent, though her powerful essence is frequently felt when she ventures nearer to the surface of my consciousness and I can feel her barely contained excitement or joy over something transpiring in the present time of my daily life.

During these times I half expect her to burst through to the fore of my consciousness and surprise the living daylights out of those around me. Once she nearly did when I had a house full of out-of-town overnight guests and the movie of Sir Arthur Conan Doyle's story of his true experience with woodland fairies came on television. In Little Self's high excitement over this movie, I literally had to muffle her exuberance as I strongly felt she was about to point to the screen and, in her little childlike voice exclaim, "Oh look, Sally, come watch! I just love this story!" Have you ever seen a small child be so excited about something that he/she literally trembles and shakes? That's the sensation I felt from Little Self's excitement over this movie. She was so bursting with excitement I could actually feel it and truly feared she would pop out at any moment while company was lounging around the living room. As our visitors began to ignore the movie with conversation, I thought for sure that Little Self would become upset and glare at them for not paying attention to something important they should see . . . and believe in.

What we know about the mechanics of Time could fit in a thimble—a fairy's thimble. What we know of the vast potentialities of the consciousness is even less. My own experiences with the technicalities of this ancient, multicultural legend is what prompted the idea for this book. It made me realize that, no matter what term you choose to characterize the phenomenon of the "trined feminine consciousness"—legend or myth—it's real. It's still real. It's very real.

Being aware of the unique consciousness of my Child Within and that of my Elder Within sparked a wild wonderment within my curious mind. If one could time-travel, couldn't one also meet one's older aspect of self from one's future? Or one's younger aspect of self from one's past? What if Time circled and coiled back on itself and crossed the past with the future where the Silver-haired Girl Child and the Crone could also meet . . . face to face while the present-day consciousness listened in and observed all that transpired between them? What might this curious encounter be like? This book is about one such speculative journey into the trined depths of the feminine consciousness—into the labyrinth of reality that some still choose to call legend.

Note: Throughout this narrative, the author's present-day consciousness—that of Mary Summer Rain of the present (the Mother Aspect)—is the story's unseen "listener and observer" hearing and observing what is transpiring between her other two companion Aspects. Therefore, during the dialogues between Little Self and the Crone, their acknowledged conversational reference to that third Aspect of the author's present-day consciousness is verbalized as "Mary" or the "Mother Aspect."

Chapter One

The floppy Raggedy Ann doll, faded fabric worn and tattered in places from receiving so many exuberant hugs, was missing one dark button eye. The other, a shiny black triangle, was chipped and in need of tightening. The doll had been carefully set down upon the leafy ground with her back propped against a well-used basket of freshly-gathered fringed sage.

Warmly falling through tall lodgepole pines, liquid gold sunshine sprinkled dappled patterns that randomly splashed onto the forest floor in rapidly spreading tide-pools of molten glitter.

High above, fathoms of ocean blue sky gave the surreal and dreamlike illusion of one being able to reach up and immerse testing fingertips into its rich depths, as it created a seemingly touchable backdrop for the brightly backlit gold and amber aspen leaves.

Gazing up through the fragile filigree of autumn foliage, the small Child's deep mahogany eyes, wide with wonder, sparkled with the reflected delicate images of nature's mesmerizing beauty. Intent on observing everything there was to see, she smiled in wonder while watching the inter-active play of dancing light and colors as they rearranged the living nature patterns with each new exhaled breath of mountain breeze. The breeze, gently blowing the patterns into shifting, swirling designs. The breeze, creating moving stained glass mosaics everywhere the Child looked.

Nature was weaving with grace.

Gliding soulfully.

Choreography, altering with nature's ever-changing depth of mood.

Like a magical kaleidoscope being gently rotated and tilted by the weathered hands of the old Woman of the Woods, the enrapt Child vividly envisioned the ageless elder blessing her with a rare, euphoric melding of each other's tender and sensitive souls. The little one deeply respected and loved her Grandmother Earth with all her heart. And throughout the whole of her young life she'd always thought of Granny Nature as being the perfect symbolic image of everything the true wise old Woman of the Woods was supposed to be.

Heady incense, the fresh pine and fir, the juniper and blue spruce, lazily wafted in thick swirling tendrils around and through the needled branches. It infused the dancing sun patterns with a heightened aura of blended magic—a powerful fairy potion permeating one's senses with joyful visions of happy things like puppy kisses, and tickling the heart with warm thoughts recalling most-loved memories.

Together, the potent fragrance and the spirit of Granny Nature joyfully joined their sweet essences to draw any and all receptive human spirits into their hypnotic dance of serenity.

Accustomed to routinely immersing herself within this tranquil enchantment of the woods, the Child was reluctant to break off the soul connection she'd made with it, and so a whispered sigh escaped from her small, bow mouth. With a measurable force of will, she voluntarily broke the soothing lull she'd allowed nature's spell to put her under.

Slowly, she sat up.

Her gaze was temporarily drawn to the wicker basket rounded high with its fragrant contents of gray-green sage before she shifted her attention to focus on the purpose of her journey to this high enchanted place, a place now seen a short distance away through the sun-dappled evergreens.

Wondering at the wiseness of coming to this particular remote forest destination, she thoughtfully took in and considered the many interesting details of the little woodland cottage just visible through the lush cover of stately evergreens.

As the late afternoon sun lazily lowered in the western sky, the Child's heart leapt to see how the orange orb's changing light washed the vine-covered cottage in a soft and rich shade of rosy alpenglow.

She smiled then.

She smiled with the thought that perhaps the warm feeling that this gentle light filled her with was a sign—a mystical signal that her trip here was indeed sanctioned by the wise Spirit Elders.

As far as she knew, no journey of this kind had ever been made or even attempted before, no such physical meeting between the separate Aspects of one consciousness had ever been physically manifested and, it seemed it was an unprecedented move on her part to even think of making such an attempt. She wasn't sure it would work. No, she wasn't sure it would work even if she timed the golden twilight moment just right.

Now, while waiting for that magic moment with butterflies flitting about in her stomach, she again studied her destination.

She'd not been disappointed at its modest size and appearance, for she knew the owner would feel most comfortable in a small dwelling. What did surprise her was that the place seemed to be the same structure that the Mother Aspect was currently residing in and, being such, wondered how this could be so? Yet there were differences between the two, differences that only the passing of time could account for.

Boston ivy, something the Mother was wanting to plant, was now donning its autumn costume of ruby red leaves as they shaded the northwest wall of the stone cottage in a blaze of brilliance.

Stone. The place was made of stone instead of the cedar she had expected to see.

Small multipaned windows sparkled their stained-glass colors between the thick frame of ivy leaves.

The gray slate roof line was broken by a chimney of river rock, giving evidence of a working fireplace or woodstove somewhere within and, high atop the roof's ridge poised a flying witch weathervane that gently moved in the breeze. This last made the Child grin in amusing remembrance as she recalled when the humorous witch had been installed back in the spring of 1999.

Beside the house were four feed bowls surrounding a stone birdbath perched atop an aspen stump. Out the back door of the cottage was a carefully tended flower garden bordered by a low redwood lattice fence. Birds of many kinds were freely helping themselves to the offerings in the seed and grain feeders on the covered front porch.

It was a good place.

It had a warm and welcoming feel to it. It was plain to see that all of nature's wild ones felt at home there because they were so openly provided for.

The Child hoped she would be too.

Noticing the altering light, she stood, then reached down to pick up her doll and basket.

Taking a deep breath, she turned to face the cottage.

And gauging the distance between it and herself, she calculated the timing to reach the dwelling's wooden back door.

Timing was of the essence now. It was critical, for this meeting could only be managed if her knock on the cottage door coincided with the precise moment of twilight when Time opened its dimensional door for those who knew how to step over its threshold.

Releasing a long, deep breath to relieve the nervousness, the Young One began to place one foot before the other as she followed the well-worn footpath that led down the hillside slope to the mountain dwelling.

The former brilliance of the alpenglow was fading.

The brightness of the Boston ivy dimmed.

Two more steps. Three.

Small fingers tightened around the basket handle.

An arm squeezed the doll closer to her heart.

Sun, disappearing below the ridgeline, cast the cottage in a new wash of grayness.

Four more steps before checking the sky.

Then five more brought her inside the garden gate.

She stole a moment to look down at the profusion of thriving blossoms. Tall purple foxglove spikes grew beside maroon and white hollyhocks. Dwarf Shasta daisies encircled the feet of a French lilac like a natural fairy ring, columbines of various colors filled the spaces between the spreading red-blossomed yarrow plants. And Johnny-jump-ups carpeted the garden soil like an Oriental rug of miniature pansy faces. Trailing up the fencing were three kinds of red, purple, and ivory-colored clematis. Wild bindweed, thick and lush, grew copiously over the lower garden fencing.

It struck the Child that all the growing plants were reluctant to succumb to the sleep that the autumn spirit was attempting to lull them into.

Trying to quell her heart's excited flutterings and the queasiness that had filled the whole of her insides, the Child softly tiptoed across the decorative flagstone walkway that led to the back steps of the cottage.

Very quietly she ascended the three wooden planks and stood squarely in front of the door. Looking first at her doll for supportive encouragement, then down at the pungent stalks of sage in the basket, she considered rearranging the greenery but then decided that she couldn't make anything more presentable than they already were.

Inhaling and exhaling several deep breaths to calm her racing heart, she glanced one last time up at the sky and scanned the forest depths to calculate the light of the woods.

It was a bit grayer now.

Time was poised. She could feel it in her bones.

Twilight had come.

The magical moment had arrived.

Blowing out her breath between pursed lips, the Child raised her hand to the door and knocked . . . once.

Nothing happened.

Disappointed, her mind raced as doubts speared in. Is this really possible? Could she really meet the wise Aspect of her Elder Self? Face to face?

She knocked a second time.

Nothing.

Was this Twilight thing just a myth after all? No, she thought with a quick shake of the head to dislodge the idea. She knew it was true. It was. It was true!

With firm conviction and greater resolve, she knocked once more.

And when the heavy wooden door slowly opened on silent hinges, the Child's deep mahogany eyes raised to look into the same deep mahogany eyes that twinkled back at her. "It is true," she whispered.

"Yesss," came a returned whisper from the old one inside, "it is true! Come in, Child, you already know that my house is yours."

The little one tilted her head before entering. "You know who I am?"

"Why, of course I do. I've been waiting a long time for you to come and visit. You're Little Self!" she said with a broadening smile. "Come in, come in! We need to get to know one another. My goodness, we've got so much to talk about, don't you think?"

Chapter Two

Eagerly entering the cottage, the little one's soft brows furrowed with questions. "But how did you know? How did you know I've been wanting to actually meet you like this, to test the Twilight Hour?"

"Ahh, because you've forgotten that I'm also the future aspect of yourself. All of this has already happened in my time. Time has just curled back a bit to cross with yours."

The Child had no problem understanding that and, without trying to appear nosy or too rude, she stood in the center of the kitchen and casually looked about. Freshly gathered herbs were hung from the cross-beams, drying and emitting a sweet mix of pleasing fragrances.

Many types of baskets hung between the tied bundles of greenery.

Homemade applesauce was simmering on the stove. The place smelled deliciously welcoming.

Sniffing the air, the youngster couldn't help but smile. "Mmmm, it reminds me of the Mother's place," she commented.

"Well, this is the Mother's place . . . in the future. You probably noticed that the garden is much the same as hers except for the addition of the hollyhocks and the advanced age of those lilac trees. They've grown tall and strong over time."

Thinking back on the garden she'd just passed by, the Child realized that it indeed was the passing of time and the age of the trees that had given the garden such a different look.

"Yes," she readily agreed, "it is the same one. I'm especially surprised to see how that wild bindweed took off! Right now, I mean, back in the Mother's time, it just took root and we didn't even know where it came from. Mother always liked climbing flowering vines and she thinks it was a gift of Nature that the vines suddenly appeared and started to grow right at the bottom of the garden fence!" The Child whispered then, "Don't you think that was strange? Don't you think that was sorta mysterious the way that wild bindweed just appeared one day in just the right place in her garden—at the bottom of the fence?"

The elder's brow arched. "Mysterious? There are no mysteries or esoteric elements to nature, Little Self. All happens as it happens, according to its own wonderful reality. If there's anything 'special' about it, it's nature's own special reality—it's own special type of inherent nature. Be careful, dear, don't go makin' mysteries where there are none to make."

The Child scrunched up her face in doubt. Then her eyes rounded. "It was a gift," she said hushed with conviction, "a gift from the fairy people. I know it was."

"Well," the Crone smiled, "perhaps it was then if you're that sure about it. Perhaps it was like the one hundred and one crows that perched in the winter aspen trees outside her bedroom window on the morning of her birthday. Huh? Do you think the appearance of the bindweed was something like that?"

The Child giggled at that thought, at the memory of the

huge flock of crows and the awe they instilled with their sudden appearance. "Ohh, yesss! I do! I think it was just like that—a gift of Nature—a special gift for the Mother. I'm also glad the lilacs she planted finally grew into big trees, because she was concerned about them making it at this elevation." She then looked deep into the elder's eyes which beamed with bright sparkles. "This is really strange, isn't it?" Then she again whispered, "like magic?"

"What's strange?"

"Us being here like this. This place, me being here in the Mother's place in a future time. You and me. You and me here like this."

"Ohhh, I don't think so. It's not so strange after you get used to the idea. Reality's quite interesting. Once you get to know it, you become quite comfortable with seeing all of its faces and moods," she confided while noticing the Child's eyes scanning the living room beyond the kitchen. "Here dear, let's give you a tour of the place so you're more at ease."

The little one took that opportunity to bring attention to the gift she'd brought with her. She proudly raised her basket up. "Look. I brought you some fresh-picked sage. I thought maybe we could bundle them up later and hang them. The Mother always does that in the fall and I figured she'd keep on doing it when she got old." The Child's cheeks flushed after realizing what she'd said. "I mean . . . when she got up in years." The flush deepened. "No, I mean, I figured you'd like doing the same thing when you—she—got . . . ."

The old one quietly chuckled to hear the little one's efforts. "It is a bit confusing, isn't it? But yes, you were quite right to think that. As you can see," she said, pointing to the rafters, "I still do that. And thank you for being so thoughtful." She reached out for the wicker handle. "Why don't we just set this basket up here on the counter for now and get to it a little later, after you've seen the place. Would that be all right?"

The youngster nodded, then followed close on the heels of the older one.

The living room had an old and comfortable familiarity to the Child. "You got a new love seat and wing chair," said the small visitor.

"Oh my, no, no. The old set was just redone, is all. The pieces had become quite threadbare and the sheepskin throws could no longer save what was left of the fabric. Had to do something to save the set. Do you like them?"

"Yes, I do. I think the Mother would like them, too. She likes that kind of fabric design. It's called, ummm, it's called . . ."

"Tapestry," the Crone filled in. "It's called tapestry."

"Yeah, tapestry. Anyway, the Mother really likes flowery designs," she said before pitching headlong into an excited barrage of trailing thoughts. "I think it comes from one of the past lives she lived in England because she can trace a whole slew of her likes for things to that time, things like pewterware and English gardens and heavily-carved dark wood furniture and ivy-covered stone cottages. She also likes plaids and that comes from the Scottish life time when . . ." The Child suddenly made a frustrated facial expression. "You're going to have to help me along here because this is really confusing. This new fabric is something the Mother will do with this furniture in her future, right?"

"Right. I think you have the necessary basics of this meeting. Give it a little time, dear. It'll only feel a bit strange until you become more accustomed to it. See," the old one said, pointing out various statuettes placed about the living room, "you'll notice that many of the Mother's familiar things are still here. Some have been given away over time and others have been added. I would think that you'd not feel like too much of a stranger here in the Mother's home-of-the-future because much of it is still the same as in her current time." The elder invitingly extended her arm in a sweeping motion. "Feel free to look about, Little Self. After all, this is your home, too. It'll possibly be your own future home where you reside with the Mother. Go ahead, feel free to look around all you want."

Hesitantly, the Child slowly moved about the room picking up familiar items and examining new ones. The scent of high mountain cedar still permeated the place. "You still burn the same incense," she noticed.

"Oh yes, once a favorite always a favorite," she smiled, following the Child into the dining area.

"Where's all the office equipment?"

"Ohhh, long gone. There's no need for any of that now. Once the Mother's books were done she gave it all away."

This surprised the Child. "Everything? Even the fax?"

The old woman nodded. "Even the fax. She liked it much better that way. It was so much quieter in the cottage after she got rid of the noisy office machinery. She never did like the fast pace of all that impersonal electronic stuff, you know. Then too, for a long while electronic equipment was useless and . . . well, I suppose that phase of reality was a part of my time and hasn't yet become one of yours and the Mother's. Much has changed since your time, Little Self. Much has changed."

The Child peered back into the living room. "The TV's gone, too?"

"Well, you knew that'd eventually go, didn't you? She rarely watched it. As you can see, she filled that corner with bookshelves. Look there," she said, pointing to the countertop, "she has a radio for keeping up on what's happening in the world. What else would she need?"

The Child's shoulders hitched up and dropped down in a shrug. "When will all these changes take place?"

"Oh slowly, in their own time they'll all happen." And within the blink of an eye the subject was changed. "Say! I bet you'd love to see the upstairs! Would you like to see that?"

The small brown eyes sparkled. "Oh yes! Could I?"

The aspen branch stair railing was still the same. So was the forest green carpeting. As the two gained the top landing, the Child noticed that the drywall she was used to seeing was covered with knotty pine paneling.

"Yes," the old one said, reading the other's thoughts, "the Mother and Sally finally did finish the place. See here?" she said, guiding the small visitor to the right of the landing. "Here's Sally's room. See how it's all finished now."

The Child respectfully stepped through the doorway and looked around. "So Sally's still with her in the future—I mean, with you?"

"Oh yes. She's out on errands today but, yes indeed, she's still with this old woman. We're still best friends and have both grown wrinkled over time." Pointing to a painting on the wall, the elder rested her hands on the child's shoulders and quietly asked, "Do you remember that picture?"

"Uh-huh, it's—was—with the stacks of artwork Sally had done over the years. I was always especially drawn to this one because well, it reminded me of what fun it is to go visit grandma." The little one's head tilted as she pensively studied the piece of art. "But," she commented, "I think this one's a little bit different than the one I'm used to seeing."

"That's because it is different. Sally redid it in the winter of 1999. It ended up being the artwork for one of the

Mother's book covers." Without expanding further on the painting, the old woman gently tapped the Child's shoulder and, with a gleam in her eye said, "Now, come see our room. I think this is the one you're most interested in."

The two crossed the hall and entered the elder's room.

Little Self stood transfixed. "Ohhh!" she cooed, "it's exactly the same."

"Well dear, not quite. Go over to your corner and see what's new."

Little Self ran to the dormer corner and picked up the Raggedy Ann doll. She compared it with the one still in her arms. "Yours is much older now, isn't it? And oh, you've added more books to my bookshelf!"

The elder had followed the Child across the room and settled herself down in the fur-draped rocker in front of the dormer window. "Oh yes," she said with eyes all atwinkle, "the Mother aspect never stopped adding your favorite titles. Would you like me to read one to you?"

The precocious Child shot the elder a long look. "I'm not a baby. I can read them myself."

"Well then, why don't you come sit on my lap and we'll look at some of these together. Would you like that or would that be too juvenile for you to do?"

The Child felt a twinge of guilt tweak her heart. "I'm only six. I'd love to do that with you if that's okay, if you wouldn't mind."

"Mind? Why would I ask such a thing if I minded. Here," she said, patting her lap, "pick a title and bring it here. We'll look at it together."

The excited Child's eyes panned along the rows of titles, all the while exclaiming over the new ones that'd been added. She stopped at one in particular. "Ohh, I love this one! Where did the Mother end up finding *Water Babies*?"

"On that old Internet thing. Actually Sally found it for

you. The Mother knew you'd like having it again. Is that the one you want to look through?"

The Child enthusiastically nodded, pulled the book from the shelf and climbed up on the old woman's lap. She reverently smoothed her small hand over the glossy cover and, as she opened to the first page, noticed the light washing over the illustration. Curious, the Child raised her head to gaze out the multipaned window at the valley beyond.

Seeing the Child's frown borne of her unspoken question, the elder clarified, "You're thinking it should be dark out by now, eh? Yet we can read by the light of Twilight, Little Self. In a way, we've stopped Time," she added while starting to put the rocker in motion. "It's holding its breath while we're here together like this. We haven't actually stopped Time, we're just . . . just caught up in a Forever Twilight while we're together."

"Oh," was all the youngster said in reply before giving her attention back to the much-loved book she'd treasured when the Mother was a child.

And together they spent a span of time reading the text and examining the book's detailed and colorful illustrations that hadn't appeared to fade over time.

When finished, Little Self gently replaced the book on the shelf exactly where she'd found it and strolled over to the north window. Nose to the pane, she commented, "I don't remember seeing this big tree when I walked up to the house. It's a maple, isn't it?"

"It is. It's been growing there for nearly forty years now."

The corners of the Child's mouth tipped up in a smile of satisfaction. "I'm glad Mother was finally able to get a maple to grow. She missed their red colors every autumn and always wanted to try to plant one outside her bedroom window. I'm really happy to know that it worked, that it could grow up here."

"Ohhh," sighed the elder, "it was touch and go there for awhile, believe me, it was touch and go. The heavy spring snows at this elevation severely tested the branches' strength, but we managed to nurse it through some of those tough times while it was maturing. It is beautiful this time of year, isn't it?"

Thoughtfully, the Child stated, "Sooo . . . that tree would've been planted around . . . uhmmm, the millennium then, or shortly after it."

The old woman beamed. "You always were a bright girl. Let's go have some of that applesauce, shall we? It should be just right by now."

Chapter Three

Sitting in the warm kitchen, the Child pensively stirred the cinnamon and sugar around in her bowl until it was completely mixed in with the cooked applesauce. She looked up into the eyes of the old woman across from her and said, "You know that my name is Little Self," she began, "and the Mother Aspect of our consciousness is Mary the author, but . . ."

"But?"

"Well, you're the elder, the wise Crone Aspect of her consciousness, but . . . but what do I call you? It seems kind of disrespectful to call you Crone even though that's what your Aspect is called." Without a moment's hesitation the Child added, "It sounds, you know . . ." She then lowered her voice and secretively whispered, "It sounds . . . witchy."

Hearing that, the old one threw back her head and broke out in an uproarious cackle. The crow's feet at the corners of her eyes merrily crinkled and her wispy silver hairs wafted about as though a magical breeze had passed through them. "Oh Child, you are a treasure! You and I both know that, in this case, the term Crone has nothing at all to do with witches. So!" she exclaimed. "You want to know what to call me. Hmmm," she mumbled while tapping her fingernails on the table, "how about using something like . . . well, something like 'Grandma' or 'Granny?' I do look like a Granny, don't I?" she said, while melodramatically fanning her gnarled fingers through the ends of the thin hair filaments for emphasis.

Little Self giggled at the unexpected antics and truthfully admitted that she did indeed look like a grandma. "Okay," she readily chirped, "I'll call you Granny, if that's all right. I don't have a real-life grandma anymore. Still, it feels a little weird calling you that because you're really an older Aspect of me—of the Mother and me." The Child cupped her hand over her mouth and giggled again at the thought. "Yeah, that's pretty funny."

"I think so too, but that's how it is, isn't it?"

"Yep, that's how it is all right," she echoed before returning her attention to the bowl of applesauce. "Mmmm, this is sooo good. Mother used to make homemade applesauce like this. I love it. And I love how it makes the cabin smell when it's cooking"

Watching the Child inhale the treat, the old one commented, "there's more on the stove if you'd like some."

"Oh, I don't want to eat it all."

"Nonsense. Here," she said, reaching for the near-empty bowl, "let me fill this back up for you."

Grandma vanished into the kitchen and quickly reappeared with a second bowl of piping hot applesauce. "It's good for you. Whenever I make this I always end up with too much because Sally doesn't especially care for it and I can't eat it all. Don't worry, Child, you're not taking food out of this old woman's mouth."

Working her way through the freshly-cooked fruit, Little Self was deep in thought trying to tie some loose elements of their meeting together.

"Granny?"

"Mmmm?"

"If that maple tree out there was planted nearly forty years ago by the Mother shortly after the millennium, is this the year 2040?"

The elder, naturally expecting such an analytical question from this wildly precocious small one, smiled. "Yes and no. It could be. Do you know why I can't give you a definitive answer to that?"

The Child quietly set her spoon down and sat back in the chair to think things out. She began by asking another question. "In the Mother's and my time it's the fall of 1999. She's almost fifty-four. In forty more years she'll be ninety-four. So . . . are you ninety-four?"

"I've always been ninety-four."

Thinking.

Waiting.

"Sooo . . . does that mean that Mother will live to be that age? Does it mean that she will reach ninety-four and that will be as old as she gets?"

"Not necessarily."

"Not necessarily," the Child thoughtfully repeated, while picking the spoon back up and stirring it around in the bowl. "Because of probabilities between the Mother's time and yours that could alter her lifespan."

"That's right. That's exactly right. You see, as the Elder Aspect of her consciousness, I've always been the old Crone of herself. I'm quite naturally an aged element of herself who holds the wisdom that she will gain through her lifetime of growing and learning. If she reaches the age of ninety-four then this place is exactly how hers will look in the year 2040 if all probabilities end up happening as they did to create this final place as you see it. Since she's still living—giving energy to her future probabilities—this place remains as is. If certain probabilities alter, this place would likewise be altered. If she should happen to exit her life tomorrow or anytime between the Then and this future time of the Now, this place will not be manifested as you see it."

The Child thought on that. She mulled it over and over in her head. "So this place is really a probability—just one probability of the Mother's future, right?"

"That's right."

"And if she moves from her current place then I would've visited you in that new one instead of this one."

The elder slapped the tabletop. "Right again!"

Silence.

The Child resumed eating her applesauce while deep in thought. After she scraped the bowl clean, she took it to the sink and rinsed it out. She returned to the table to wait for the old one to finish eating and then rinsed out the second bowl. Standing at the sink she spied the basket of greenery. She turned to the elder and asked, "wanna bundle up this sage now?"

The elder smiled to herself as she rose from her chair.

"I think that's a wonderful idea. The twine's in the same place it's always been. Why don't you get it out and I'll bring the scissors."

The Child went straight to the right drawer and pulled out the ball of twine while the old one met her at the kitchen counter with the scissors.

"You picked these at just the right time," the elder complimented.

"Mother taught me that. She picks fresh sage in the early fall while the buds are still green. That way they don't fall apart and make a big mess in the house. She hangs them from her kitchen and living room rafters. I love the smell of them," she said before hesitating to say the rest. "Of course, you already know all that, don't you? You already know everything that the Mother does and will do in life."

"Yes, I already know all that." The elder peered down at the Child. "Does that upset you?"

"No, it doesn't upset me; it just brings so many questions to my mind. I want to ask about Mother's future and the world's future but I don't think that'd be right—appropriate."

"Is that a statement or are you asking a question? Are you asking me if that'd be appropriate for you to ask about? Are you fishing?"

The Child sheepishly grinned. "Maybe. I don't know. I wanna do what's right. I know there are rules for this kind of thing and I've always tried to stay within the spiritual law of stuff like this.

"When I first appeared to the Mother's friend I wanted to blurt out so much to her, but I knew I couldn't—shouldn't. I tried just giving her teeny tiny hints about things, but she ended up guessing so much from them that . . . well. I could only say so much and then had to hold myself back from revealing more than I was supposed to." The Child made a face. "It's not fun getting in trouble with the High Spirit Ones."

"Well," said the elder, smiling with reassurance, "as I recall of that time, you did just fine." She chuckled, "Your exuberance did runneth over some, but you were too connected to the Otherside to go beyond the limits you knew were there. Same applies now, Little Self, same applies now. Though I'd like to tell you all that happens in Mother's future and that of the world's between 1999 and 2040, I can only give subtle indications, maybe a few specifics here and there, but nothing more than that."

"I know," sighed the young one, "I know the rules and I sure wouldn't expect you to bend them either."

As they worked together to separate out the stalks of sage into neat bundles and wrap the twine around the stems, the two were each lost in their own separate thoughts while a warm and companionable silence wrapped snugly around them like a down quilt.

The old one spoke first. She spoke softly. "I think this is nice. I think this is so nice that you and I have finally met like this. I like spending a span of time with you."

The Child's eyes looked up into the older one's. They were misted. "Me too, Granny. I like it too."

The elder sighed. "You like it but you also don't like it, eh? You like it that we're together like this, getting to know one another, but you don't like it that you have so many questions about the future that, because of the spiritual law on that issue, I'm restrained from telling. Is that it?"

"I guess so."

"Mmmm, I thought so."

The two worked on in that warm silence before the old one whispered, "I'm no stranger to you, Little Self. You've always been a part of me, you know. I've always been a part of you, too."

The Child's hands stopped their busyness as the dynamic import of what the old one had said hit home. She looked up into the gleaming, deep amber eyes that twinkled with an implied secret newly revealed. The little one smiled wide and whispered back. "Yes! Yes! I get it! We're aspects of each other. If I'm now in 2040, I've lived through those years with the Mother—with you!"

The old woman continued wrapping the fragrant sage stalks without a moment's break in her rhythm. She hadn't actually broken any rules by giving the Child the hint because it was a simple fact of reality that the little one hadn't made the connection to yet. In time, the elder knew, the Child would've made the association all on her own.

"Be careful, Little Self," the elder cautioned, "use wisdom while looking at all those new memories you're finding in your head. Remember that they're all connected to specific probabilities happening in the past. Each event you now recall hinges on the actualization of many probabilities that manifested in the past. This place—this cottage—is not as solid as it may seem. You'll find that it's susceptible to alterations as events are occurring in the Mother's present time frame."

The Child nodded. "I understand that. The view of the future is always fluct . . . fluct . . ."

"Fluctuating," the Crone kindly filled in.

". . . fluctuating because current events make it like my colorful kaleidoscope. If Mother died back in her time while you and I were here, we'd be suddenly gone and this place would then belong to someone else and wouldn't be filled with the scents of your cedar incense, our bundled sage, and cooked applesauce."

"That's right. So when you get around to looking at those memories that are now in your mind, remember that they're just tentative ones until the Mother's present time matures to 2040 and she actually does reach the age of ninety-four."

"Granny?"

"Yes?"

"I don't think I want to look at all those memories right now. I really like being here with you like this. Can I wait to look at those memories until after I leave?"

The old one was deeply moved by the youngster's desire to spend her mental energies on the present. She knew the Child was bursting with curiosity about all that had happened to the Mother and the world in those forty years, but was heartfully touched that the Child also didn't want to waste a minute of their visit on past world events. She knew that the Child hadn't made a secondary realization regarding her decision and so decided to let the situation unfold naturally.

"Of course, Child. Of course you can wait. You've made me feel good to know that you don't want to spend our time together talking about past world history." Then the old one lifted the Child's chin. "You've done a sweet, sweet thing, Child. You've made me feel loved." And the two hugged one another.

"I do love you, Granny. I've seen how you've guided the Mother with your wisdom, with your patience, and your inner strength. I've noticed how you've given her inspiration and encouragement when life got tough for her. I love you so much for all you've done through the years."

"Oh, now, now," the elder said, patting the Child's small back. "That's my job, you know. All women have an Elder Within. Problem is, most don't know it. Besides," she tenderly added with a soft smile, "in your own special way, you've done the same thing for the Mother."

Little Self pulled back from the hug and squeezed the old one's arms. "Maybe the Mother could write a book about that some day! Right now she's thinking about it but is going back and forth about doing it because she thinks most people wouldn't understand it—the concept of it and . . ." Then the Child's eyes suddenly widened into plate-sized orbs. "Oh no! Oh yes! She does do the book, doesn't she! That artwork upstairs is going to be . . . is . . . was . . . the cover! Oh Granny, I'm so glad she went ahead and really did it!"

The elder grinned. "Me too. I'm very glad she set aside her concerns and opted for reality instead of letting public opinion smother her creativity and sense of purpose. That sense of purpose was always the mainstay that's gotten her through most of her roughest times. Though . . ."

The Child waited for the old one to finish her thought and, when she waited longer than a respectful amount of time, asked, "Though what?"

Silence.

"Did she still call the book *Keepers of the Soul*?"

"No, no she didn't. It was called *Trined in Twilight*."

The Child's forehead wrinkled and her nose scrunched up. "That's an odd title. I'm not sure I like it. And anyway, I don't even get it."

"Well!" exclaimed the elder, gathering up her bundles of wrapped sage. "Let's hang these, shall we?" came the change of subject. "You take your three and put them up wherever you can find room. I'll get the hammer and nails for the hooks."

The young one was sharp enough to recognize when the door to a subject had been closed and so she gathered up her bundles of sage to roam the cottage in search of just the right places to hang each of them. "Does it have to be from the rafters?" she called to the old one, who was still in the kitchen gathering the tools.

"Oh no, no. Wherever you want, Little Self. You ought to know we've no set rules for this kind of thing. Stick them anywhere. Wherever you find wall space that you think they'd look good on, go for it. We're not particular."

And for the next twenty minutes or so, while the Crone hummed an uncertain tune beneath her breath and the Child tested this place and that, the two had a grand time busying themselves placing the sage about the dwelling. The fresh scent of new sage wafted from every room.

When done, the old woman sidled up beside the Child. "That was very thoughtful, you know," she said while smoothing the part on Little Self's head with her gnarled hand. "I hadn't made it out for my annual gathering this year; guess I'm finally feeling my age a bit more than I'd like to admit to these days. It always seemed that it was nature itself that kept me going, kept me young—inside." She grinned with a wink. "Inside I'm still thirty-something, you know."

The Child took the hand and sweetly traced her small fingers over the weathered skin. "Oh no! Inside you'll always be twenty-something!"

Flicking her free hand in a dismissive manner, the Crone laughed with amusement, "Ohhh, you are a little imp!" But then, then the Grandmother's mood swiftly turned serious. She looked down at the small hand covering her own and studied it. And bending her head to tenderly brush it with a kiss, said, "Maybe, maybe I'll always be twenty-something inside, maybe even six!" The simple expression emotionally affected her more than she'd expected. The lump in her throat took her by surprise and, in an effort to cast it away, she quickly altered the sensitive mood. Suddenly the Crone pointed to the window and exclaimed, "Look! The bucks are here!"

Little Self's face brightened. She raced to the window and curled her feet beneath herself on the love seat. Nose to the glass, she sighed a whisper, "So they still come."

"Oh, yes," replied the elder in a return whisper as she settled herself beside the young one, "generation after generation they've brought their young. This place has become a real wildlife sanctuary over the years. And it all started back in 1996 when the Mother and Sally bought the place—when they began feeding the wild critters of every kind. You'll see," she reminded, "in a little while, the raccoons will be climbing all over the porch, just like they do back in your own time. Though many things in the world change, some things never change except to just get better—develop a history—a tradition."

Keeping her wondering eyes on the six-point bucks, the Child quietly responded, "I think this is a very special tradition," she said, noticing that the deer had just recently shed their velvet. "Do the bears still come around too?"

"Oh yes! Indeed they do. Every species seems to take

their turn here. Last week a mama bear came with her cub and it made us laugh to see it swinging from the birdbath and then do tumbling tricks over the grass around and around its mother's feet. What was even more pleasing for us to realize about the sight was that the mother was comfortable enough to bring her cub, especially since she's seen us out and about enough to know there're humans living here."

The Child looked to the old one. "Mother says that there are always eyes on us. She says that when we think we're all alone out there, we never really are, because there's always some critter or little being watching us."

"That's true. That's absolutely true. When I go out and collect the feed bowls and take them inside the garden gate to refill them with sweet feed, I can feel the deers' presence up in the woods. They're watching me put out fresh grain and it doesn't take long for them to know that that's what I'm doing for them. Most times I talk to them while I'm going about the business of resupplying their feed."

The little one smiled. "Back in my time, the Mother can go out while they're still feeding and refill their bowls without the bucks being frightened away. And whenever Sally walks out after dark to fill up the bowls, the biggest buck will let her pass within ten or twelve feet of him while he waits for her to finish!" The Child dropped her mouth in awe. "That is so cool!" Then she expanded on it. "When that first happened, when the big buck just stood there so close to Sally, the Mother was watching from the window and had to hold her breath, she was so concerned. She was afraid the buck would hurt Sally—they've been known to do that, you know. There'd been news reports about a hiker being gored by a deer. But our buck wouldn't ever do anything like that. He knew better, didn't he. He was just anxious to get back at that fresh grain. He got so big over the years that Sally called him 'Big Boy.'" The Child was proud to add, "All the wildlife around their cabin know that it's a safe place for them to hang out."

"And it will only get better from there," the elder reassured. "The wild ones have a knowing, you know. They have very strong instincts and acute intuitive senses. They naturally know which humans to trust. They watch from the treeline as the Mother and Sally go about their outside chores. They familiarize themselves with their routine activities such as tending to the garden, cutting firewood, and gathering puffballs. They come to recognize those same humans whenever they're out and about. Oh yes," Grandma emphasized, "the Mother is indeed right about there always being eyes on you. You're never alone out in those woods. Never."

Their attention again returned to the activity beyond the window. There were seven bucks now.

The Child frowned. "Ohhh," she scolded, "look how the bigger ones use their hoofs to chase away the smaller ones. I don't like it when they rake the littler one's backs like that."

"Like it or not, that's why the Mother began putting out so many bowls—so they all could have space to feed. That 'chasing off' thing the deer do is just part of nature, Little Self. There's always a pecking order, you know."

"Well, yes, I know that, but sometimes the smaller ones don't even get to eat."

"You think so? Not really, they come back later on. These animals feed off and on all night long. You just don't see them doing it because you're in bed.

"Anyway, this pecking order has a reason. Though, to someone like yourself, it may not seem to have rhyme or logic, but it does. It surely does. It teaches the younger ones respect for their elders. It teaches them to be assertive as they grow and mature. It teaches them independence. In the wild, life is always a continuing learning experience that enhances the unique survival techniques specific to each species. What may look like cruel behavior to you may, in reality, just be a natural teaching/learning experience for the species—a normal way to instruct the younger ones on how to best survive."

"Kinda like Tough Love," suggested the Child. "I never looked at it quite like that before."

"There's always different ways of seeing things, always different ways of seeing," the old one reminded, while pointing back to the window. "Look, the deer are all looking at something."

The Child gave her attention to the deer. "The raccoons! I bet they're all looking at the raccoons! They're here!"

Quickly crossing the room, Little Self kneeled up on the cedar chest beneath the picture window and peered out to spy a mother raccoon and her three babies happily eating from the overflowing bowls of food on the front porch. Their rollicking antics brought giggles and, when one baby got up on its hind legs to look back, the Child responded. "Hi, baby! You're safe here." Then she realized that these same raccoons were probably the result of many generations of animals coming to feed on this very porch since the Mother and Sally bought the place forty-four years ago. The Child looked to the old one. "I didn't have to tell them they're safe here, did I?"

"No, but it never hurts to reinforce such sentiments. They don't need to understand your words, it's the tone of voice and the gentleness of your aura that they sense and respond to."

For a while the two sat side-by-side and watched the furry, roly-poly family feed and interact with one another.

Eventually, after the critters were satiated, they each chose a particular spot on the porch to lounge in. Two babies nestled themselves in the sunflower seed trough that spanned the length of the porch rail. Their sense of beingness was so secure that they instantly fell asleep with little legs dangling down over the sides. The third baby curled up in the large feeder attached to the porch pole and swiftly fell asleep while mother kept her awareness honed to all sounds coming from down below in the nearby woods.

Little Self whispered, "The raccoon mothers are good mothers, aren't they, Granny."

"Oh yes, they surely are. They never let their guard down while caring for their young'uns."

The Child sighed. "It seems to me that that's a very frantic way to live. To have to always be on the lookout for predators leaves little time for rest or having fun. Look how she's constantly listening and then running to the edge of the porch, looking out into the woods."

"Uh-huh, I see. Yes, that's true, but while she's here—while she's got all her babies safe here—she only has to watch one direction. When she and her babies are out in the woods she has to not only watch her back but also all sides. This porch does let her relax some. It gives her more respite than you might think."

"I suppose," came the soft reply, "still."

"That's life, Little Self. Even people need to be ever aware and watchful. Not so much from without really, but from within. They need to watch their actions and thoughts in a constantly monitoring manner. They too need to guard their words and check their intentions."

The Child frowned. "That reminds me of something that recently went on in my own time. The Mother almost gave up writing the rest of her books because of what she saw happening on some of those Internet message boards.

People were twisting her words so bad that she didn't see any reason to continue writing more of them. She saw so much ignorance and meanness that she even took three of her working manuscripts off the computer. *Keepers of the Soul* was one of them. Well . . ." she corrected, "at that time, that's what she'd titled it."

"Yes, I know. I remember that, but there were two sides to this coin. She also realized that she couldn't let the more spiritually aware and intelligent readers down by not finishing the messages." The old one's voice was soft.

"You know that there will always be those people in the world who simply have to twist the words of another, who have some dark inner compulsion to search for hidden meanings behind what others say or write, or falsely convince themselves that a writer is making implied meanings from the simplest statements when none were ever intended. There will always be those kinds of people out there, Dear. Even now, in my day, after all the suffering and changes that the world's been through and experienced, some people still don't get it.

"Yes," she then said in joyous recall, "the Mother did put every one of those works-in-progress back on the computer and ended up publishing them after she remembered those special readers who had written her expressing how much those words meant to them. It was due to those aware readers like Rita and Lisa, Chris, Tee, and Debbie, it was those like Kristi, Shirley, and Kelley. It was each one of them who, unknowingly, picked the Mother back up and gave her the determination to push onward."

Little Self giggled then. "Yeah," she said, "the Mother thought of those nice people and then her hackles of determination stood straight up on end when she realized that it was them and all the thousands like them in the world that she was here for. She got really indignant then and . . ."

Suddenly shooting her fists to each side of her waist, the youngster theatrically emulated the Mother. "And she said that 'those ignoramuses of the world were not going to dictate when the writing phase of her purpose ended—they were not going to cut her messages off at the knees!' So," Little Self relaxed with a satisfied smile, "so she put the books back on the computer and ignored those dummies forever after. She never ever again logged onto the Internet. She never ever read a single message board again."

The Child pursed her lips then. "But Sally did. Sally sometimes peeked at what folks were saying and she'd get all riled and want to put in her two cent's worth after seeing how off-base people were when they twisted the Mother's words. But the Mother always told Sally to let it go, that there were people all over the world with different opinions, that what Sally saw on those message boards was just a tiny fraction of diverse opinions. Sally stayed out of it—completely off the boards—but she still didn't like what she saw going on."

Grandma nodded knowingly. "Well, that's exactly what I meant about people needing to watch their own Within. They need to realize how hurtful and damaging their thoughtless comments can be to others, how those same words and heartless comments could actually change the course of another's life or destiny. Life is just loaded with selfish intentions that externalize themselves through plain meanness. Some folks don't take the time to think about how their words could injure another—some just plain don't care.

"A good example was after the Mother so light-heartedly mentioned in *Eclipse* that she'd run out in the moonlit snowfall and danced in her bare feet on occasion. But some people couldn't take that statement at face value, they had to take that simplistic act of 'reaping joy from nature' and make ugly assumptions that she was actually implying that it was an 'act of a goddess'—likened to walking on water." The elder released a heavily weighted sigh. "Ohhh, Little Self, do you recall how utterly ridiculous the Mother thought that presumption was? How deeply grieved she was over how easily people twisted her words?"

The Child sadly nodded, listening to Grandma continue to speak from her heavy heart.

"She was deeply appalled and became justifiably angry over how something so simple as that could be twisted so out of shape into something she never intended. She was utterly flabbergasted, utterly dumbfounded, and quite speechless to understand or explain how anyone could take something so beautiful and innocent and turn it into ugliness and such a complete untruth.

"Oh yes, dear, I've watched the Mother all these years work very hard to carefully word the messages as simply as she could, so nobody could misinterpret them or get beneath them and shift them into something they weren't, but it'd always happen anyway, no matter how careful she was, it'd always happen anyway.

"So then, this is why it's so important for people to stop thinking that their dangers will be coming from somewhere Without when, in truth, they must always be on the watch for what's coming from the Within of themselves and understand the true why's of actions taken and words spoken, else they walk a false path of self-devised illusion, whereby their feet never truly touch down on reality's solid ground."

The old woman's eyes shifted to the watchful mother on the porch. "Just like that mama raccoon out there who has to continually be on the watch for predators from without, people have to watch for their own predators lurking within themselves."

"Ego is a false road, one of self-delusion," was all the perceptive Child muttered in response. More wasn't needed, for her statement definitively concluded the issue of why folks felt the continual need to criticize others.

"Oh!" the Child suddenly laughed with true joy. She pointed to the window. "Look at that baby stretch and yawn! Oh Granny," she yearned, "don't you ever wish you could just go out there and hug them? The Mother always has the urge to do that."

"But she doesn't, does she, because she knows it'd disturb their rest and relaxed family time together."

"Still, I'd like to go hug them and hold them in my arms like a baby doll. Their new fur makes them look so soft and cuddly." The youngster immediately recalled a related issue from her own time. She shared it with Grandma. "Sally and the Mother go to a wildlife lady's place near them, who has a big walk-in pen holding orphaned raccoon babies." The Child frowned as she made a disgusted face. "Men shoot the babies' mothers, you know. They shoot them thinking that the babies will die then."

"Yes, I know, Honey. I know that and I'm sorry things like that happen."

The Child continued. "Me, too. Anyways," she brightened, returning to her initial thought. "When you go inside this lady's raccoon enclosure the babies crawl all over you, they're just like excited and playful puppies!

"The lady also has pens for orphaned and injured fawns, but we can't go into that one because the fawns are very fragile. The wildlife place is where Sally and Mother took the injured prairie falcon Sally found in the road." The little one's eyes lit up. "I think it'd be fun to be a wildlife person and nurse all the injured animals back to health but, it's a very big responsibility, you know."

"It certainly is," Grandma wholeheartedly agreed. "It's

no part-time job, that's for sure. You're a caregiver for patients who can't tell you where it hurts and you have to be there all the time to monitor their changing behavior and watch for signs of declining health while they're all recuperating. It is a very big responsibility and not everyone has the patience or the love in their hearts to pull it off with the dedication required. Those who do are special people—very special people."

The Child was anxious to tell about how she'd indirectly helped the wildlife lady. "Know what?" she excitedly asked.

"What?"

"Once we, I mean the Mother and Sally, went down to Colorado Springs on an errand for the wildlife lady. We picked up some hurt animals that a veterinary hospital in Old Colorado City was holding for a special pickup to take back up the Pass to her. We picked up a teeny baby bunny and three injured birds. They were in four separate little boxes. I," the Child blushed, "I mean Mary, held them all on her lap in the pickup while Sally drove back up the mountain to the lady's place. It was lots of fun! I felt really good inside knowing that we'd helped the lady help those little hurt critters." Then a frown came like a shadow across her face. "Granny?"

"Hmmm?"

"Would it be wrong for me to sometimes wish the Mother's job was with wildlife instead of with writing books—with bringing messages to people? Sometimes, well . . . a lot of times, I think she kinda wishes that too."

Grandma tilted her head. "Why would you think that thought might possibly be wrong, Child? Working with the innocent animals of earth would certainly be much less stressful. There'd be no twisting of words, no assumptions made, no cruel or hurtful gossip. Oh, yes, I can understand you and her sometimes wishing to be working with the innocents and the pure of heart, but that's just not the way of things this time around."

Moved by the girl's deep love of, and sincere caring for animals, the Crone gently touched the other's shoulder and ran her hand down the soft, warm fabric of the Child's flannel shirt. "Don't you worry, honey, you'll do a lot more of that kind of thing during your life. You have a lot of those 'warm feelings' coming from interacting with wildlife to experience yet." She gave the Child a gentle, understanding smile. "Believe me, I know. I know because I've seen."

The Child grinned wide in anticipation. "Really? Ohhh, Granny, I hope so," she said, giving the raccoons one last look before they both crossed the room and settled into their former places on the love seat.

"That's a real comfy outfit you have on," the old one commented.

The girl looked down at her denim bib overalls that were worn soft from many launderings. "They're good for climbing trees!" she quickly informed. "And they work best for keeping my shirt tucked in." Then she leaned forward to touch the equally worn fabric of the other's long skirt. "I see you still like the skirts."

"Ah-ha," the Crone chuckled, "what else would an old mountain woman like me wear? Jeans? Those things were okay in the Mother's day, but this old lady is so much more comfortable in her skirts—they're really me, you know. They suit me perfectly." She then gave a mischievous smile, "Besides, they save on running around looking for a dust-cloth! These old skirts are mighty handy wearables and have so many uses. I even use the front to hold the kindling I collect while walking back from the woods! Kindling, pinecones, puffballs, you name it. Old age has its advantages; you learn efficiency. Why lug along some cumbersome carry-all when a skirt will serve the same purpose?" The bright eyes twinkled like a gnome's. "I wear mine!"

The Child's jaw dropped. "The Mother does that, too! I've seen her dust off furniture with her skirt. She does that all the time because the dirt roads make a lot of house dust. And she always uses the front of her skirt as a big pocket to carry back all kinds of really cool finds from the woods. Humph," Little Self finalized, "guess she's—you've—been doing that for a long time, huh."

The elder's face crinkled up like an elf's as she grinned wide. "Guess I have. Guess some old habits never die."

"Guess not," responded the Child giving a return smile before turning pensive.

Chapter Four

Silence would've hung like a mountain mist between them if it wasn't for the metered ticking of the Black Forest cuckoo clock on the wall.

The youngster's voice was heavy with childlike concern when she voiced her next thought. "You don't have a dog?"

Grandma's head tipped to one side, wisps of silver hair wafted about her face like a radiating aura. "Does that surprise you, Dear?"

"Sure it does. You've . . . the Mother . . . always had at least one dog in the house; most times you've had several."

The elder then released a long, extended sigh. "Ohhh, well. We just don't have any anymore."

That response didn't come anywhere close to satisfying the curious Child. "But why, Granny?"

Realizing the youngster wasn't going to leave the subject alone, the elder again sighed as she freely opened one of the doors of her heart. "One wearies so . . . one wearies so of losing them, Little Self. The heart can only take so much heartache from loving deeply and then having that love crushed by death.

"After a time I thought that my little furry companions would outlive me, but that never happened, I outlived them. This old heart grew tired of digging their little graves."

The Child's face fell into a sorrowful expression as she gently rested her hand over the aged one. "Ohhh," she moaned, "I'm . . . I'm sorry. I've touched on a painful subject." She patted the wrinkled hand. "I understand. Back in my time the Mother had to put her keeshond, Cheyenne, to sleep and it was sooo hard for her. She doesn't think it's fair that dogs don't have the same life span as people do. Neither do I."

"Ahhhh well, dear," Granny managed with an accepting smile, "that's just one of those misfortunes of life, isn't it?"

"Misfortune? Misfortune!" Little Self repeated with a gasp. "If you're asking me what I think, I'd say it was a whole lot more than just misfortune, it was one of God's big mistakes—a huge mistake!" She flung out her arms for emphasis. "Huge! I don't think He spent nearly enough time thinking that one out. Seems to me that, if His compassion is supposed to be so great, He'd never purposely create a situation that caused people that kind of sadness in their lives."

"Now, now, Little Self, let's not place blame."

"I'm not," the Child quickly defended. "I'm just getting to the root of it. God didn't think it out. Plain and simple," she declared.

Thin shoulders shrugged. "Perhaps," came the soft reply. "Perhaps He didn't figure on people and their dogs sharing such a deep relationship of the heart."

"Granny?"

"Yes?"

"That wasn't the real reason for why you don't have a dog now, was it? I mean, that wasn't the deeper meaning."

Grandma eyed the young one. "Tsk-tsk, you're way too smart for those little Oshkosh britches of yours. You're right. You're very perceptive. No, at least that wasn't the only reason.

"The love of a dog and the faithful companionship it gives is, well . . . it's very special and precious. It's incomparable to all other types of love, because it's love that is completely unconditional, without a shred of ego or alternative agenda attached as happens most times with human love. That pure-of-heart type of love and warm companionship is a blessing I've always treasured throughout this long life of mine. And having that deeply cherished love through the years was always, always well worth the pain of losing it at some point. That love far out-balanced the final loss I knew would one day come. But you're right, there is a deeper reason." She looked the Child in the eye. "Now I don't have a dog because I'm the one who will be leaving.

"Little Self, have you ever—well, yes, I guess you have seen many of the same things I have. Do you recall when the Mother's dear friend died and left that little dog behind?"

The Child reluctantly nodded at the sad memory.

"And do you remember how that little dog refused to eat? How it whimpered by Julia's bed all night long and had its nose to the window all day watching for her to come home? Poor little thing ended up dying from a broken heart because it didn't understand where it's human companion went. I've seen it happen time and time again.

"Well, now I'm the one who'll be going away before my pet would and I don't want to do that to a dear, loving friend who wouldn't understand where I've gone or why. I could not bring myself to cause a precious little heart that kind of grief or watch it pine away for me."

The Child blinked away the stinging behind her eyes. "So now the tables are turned. But," she offered as an alternative probability, "what if you live to be one hundred and ten years old?"

"Ohhh, Little Self," the elder soothed in a grandmotherly fashion while patting the small hand, "don't you see what you're doing? Now you're reaching. Honey, you're reaching far into improbabilities to hide the real reason behind your statement. To hope that I'd live that long is beyond logic. I think the idea of me doing that would really be pushing the envelope, don't you?"

The Child, tightly holding onto her desperate hopes, imperceptibly shook her head.

"You're in denial, Little Self. You've got to be reasonable here and not choose to deny the reality of things." The old woman sighed. "Oh, Dear Heart, look at me. This old head of silver has gotten so thin and wild that it looks more like wispy fairy hair." Slowly extending her hands in front of the girl and splaying fingers that were no longer straight, she compassionately asked, "do these honestly look like hands that will actually age another fourteen years?"

The Child refused to look. It wasn't that she was being obstinately defiant, it was because she knew in her heart that the Crone was right and that the truth of her words lodged firmly in her chest like a hard, cold stone. And so it was that her heart chose to completely ignore the reality her mind knew was being displayed before her. "Maybe," she finally whispered, "maybe they do. Maybe they look like hands that will live for fourteen more years to gather puffballs, kindling, and make applesauce."

Grandma continued holding her hands out. "You didn't look," she reminded. "You didn't even look."

When the Child's eyes rose to lock on the elder's, they first skimmed over the hands. Then, "Why?" she asked. "Why am I reaching? Unless, of course, you just plain don't want to live to be that old."

The wise old woman recognized a rationalization when she heard it. "Oh, as long as I'd still have my health and could still get around by myself I suppose I wouldn't mind, but I always factor in all possible probabilities, you know. No, so far I've been lucky, but at this age I think it's wise not to push that envelope and want more. I've been blessed with reasonably good health so far and I feel gratefully blessed by it. But," she cautioned, bringing the subject back to the important issue of the Child's denial, "Little Self, you have to look at your fear, look it square in the face and say its name."

The Child bowed her head. "Why?"

"Why? Because if you don't you'll always be scavenging around for someone else to blame for it, that's why."

Thinking.

Waiting.

"Okay!" Little Self angrily blurted out. "So I'm reaching! I'm reaching for the tiny ray of hope that you'll live for another fourteen years because . . ." Small eyes glistened. "Because I don't want you to ever die! There! There, I looked it in the face and said its name. I have a fear of the Mother dying!" She didn't want Granny to soothe or comfort her because that kind of compassion would only plunge her into deeper sadness and make it worse.

Knowing how the Child felt, the Crone held tightly to the reins of her emotional instincts to comfort the youngster. She merely furrowed her brows in empathy while Little Self talked herself out of her sorrow.

The Child worked her fingers as they fidgeted with the fabric of her front pocket. Her eyes stayed downcast while she talked it out. "You were right. I know that's not the point, but I want you to know that I know you were right. I do have a fear of the Mother dying. I want her to live to complete all the work she came to do and I want her to live to enjoy a good, long life afterward. I was trying to blame you for facing the reality I wanted to deny. I'm sorry," she said, sniffing. "I was wrong to do that. I really didn't mean to do that."

"I know that, Honey. I know," the Crone whispered.

"Well . . . just so you know, that's all," concluded the Child as she wiped her eyes with her frayed sleeve.

Granny decided it was time to return the conversation to its initial subject matter. "About getting that dog . . . I'm fine with my decision, Little Self. Don't worry on my account. I still have plenty of companionship. My goodness," she smiled, "I've got the deer, coons, birds, and all the other little people of the woods." Grandma winked, "Oh yes, lots of other little people."

The Child didn't catch the hidden meaning. "Yes, but you always loved your dogs so much," she reminded. "You always took such comfort from them—and they from you. Think how having another little furry person around the house would liven things up, be warm and cuddly in your bed at night, and kiss away your tears." Little Self absent-mindedly cast her eyes about the floor. As if searching for something. "I couldn't figure out what was missing from this place when I first walked in until I realized that there were no little four-leggeds rushing up to greet me, no food bowls in the kitchen corner, no doggie toys strewn about the floor. Oh Granny," she cried, "won't you think about it? Please, please won't you think about it?" she pleaded. "Please?"

Granny sighed. "Did you come here just to pester me, Child?"

The impatient youngster ignored the question. "Will you promise me that you'll think about it after I leave? Please? Will you at least do that?"

"Did you not hear anything I just got through saying about this subject?"

"Of course I heard. I listen very well and I heard—and felt—a lot more than what was said. That's why I'm asking you if you'll at least think about it some more. Please, please, please!"

"Child, you are persistent, aren't you."

The little one's head eagerly bobbed up and down in reply.

"Mmmm," Granny hummed in deliberation while raising a teasing brow. "If I promise, will that shut you up?"

The Child giggled and gave a sharp salute. "Yes, ma'am!" she shot back. "Yes, Ma'am!"

"Okay," the Crone chuckled, "then I promise."

Little Self gave Granny a long suspicious look out of the corner of her eye. "You're not just saying that, are you?"

Displaying feigned shock, "Would I do that? Moi?"

The Child narrowed her eyes, pretending to think on that. Waiting.

Then, "No, Granny, you wouldn't do that."

The old woman reached down and patted the Child's knee. "I'm glad you know that."

"Well . . . I know the Mother and, you wouldn't be any different than her. Your philosophy would be just the same as hers. Your word is just as good."

"Tell me, Little Self, why is this so important to you?"

"Why is what so important to me?"

"The deal with the puppy, Silly. The puppy."

"I'm not sure; it just is."

"Well, then," said the Crone with surety, "then I promise I'll give it some deeper thought."

"Granny?"

"Hmmm?"

The Child smiled wide. "Thank you."

The elder thoughtfully ran the Child's long braids through her gnarled fingers. And winked. "You're very welcome . . . I think."

Chapter Five

The two on the love seat returned their attention to the feeding bucks and watched their antics before Little Self voiced a question.

"Do you mind if I ask a couple of questions?"

"As the Mother always says, 'You can always ask but the answer may not be what you expect to hear.'"

The Child suppressed a smirk. "Oh, I'm never in expectation, Granny. I learned that a long time ago. My question is about the abbey idea that the Mother is thinking about building. Did it ever come into being?"

The elder's eyes brightened. "Oh, yes! It sure did. Why? Did you have doubts about it?"

"Well, back in my—the Mother's—own time, she's having some problems. You know, with finances, and it's touch and go each month. I just wondered if all that worked out so she could get on with the plans for the abbey?"

"You're wondering if the idea ever got to the stage where it became a lot more than just an idea. It did. It surely did. Necessity made the Mother and Sally very creative and they worked hard together to get their bills paid off. They sold personal possessions, worked several jobs and continued making the metal sculpture pieces in their basement workshop.

Eventually everything worked out. Yes, Little Self, everything came into being in its own time. It all came about through innovative creativity, hard work, and determination."

The young one blew out a breath. "That's a relief." Then another question came from her lips. "Did the public controversy about it go away?"

"Oh, my, you're bringing back a lot of old memories. Let's see . . . Yes, as I recall, that controversy was due to people's assumptions about the abbey. They didn't understand what it was all about and imagined all sorts of presumptive ideas regarding the reason for it. The Mother and Sally ignored them all, though. They had their hands full at the time. They were far too busy working at those extra jobs and caring for Sally's mother to give any mind to what was being said or assumed.

"There was a bit of trouble for a time, though. After the abbey was built it was vandalized several times."

The Child didn't seem surprised to hear that. "Oh, no," she moaned, "I suspected something like that would happen, but you know what I thought was really odd?"

"What's that, Dear?"

"I thought it was really odd that the idea of the abbey being vandalized never came into the Mother's mind. I mean, she never even thought of it as a possibility or a slim probability. It never once crossed her mind to think people would do such things. Especially to a secluded spiritual sanctuary." The youngster's head shook. "She's such an optimist . . . almost to a fault. Don't you think she's an incurable optimist?"

"Optimist? Oh, yes. To a fault? Little Self," the old woman was sure to caution, "optimism is never a fault unless it becomes one viewed through those silly rose-colored glasses and the Mother never ever put those on—never even owned a pair in her entire life."

"Still," the Child insisted, "being aware of church bombings and such during her time, you'd think the thought would naturally be in the back of her mind, at least as a possibility. It never was."

"No, not until it happened the first time."

"Did she take it hard?"

"You know her as well as I do. Sure she did. Yet she, Sally, and some of their friends went out there and worked together to set things right again. Every time it was vandalized they repaired the damages. Finally the destruction stopped."

"It just stopped? Just like that?"

Nodding, the Crone happily declared, "Yes, just like that."

With relief, the Child responded, "I'm glad to know that. Seems to me that it'd be really discouraging."

"Of course, it was, but you know those two. Besides," she added with a new twinkle in her eye, "by then they had quite a few supportive womenfolk who'd offered their services as volunteers! You know, like offering to check up on the chapel from time to time, keep the place picked up, do simple repairs. Bet you never figured on that happening, did you?"

Little Self cocked her head. "I dunno." Then, shaking the braids in animated answer, said, "No, I don't think it ever occurred to me," she said, "nor to the Mother or Sally, either. Right now, back in my time, Mary and Sally are thinking that they're going to have to build it and take care of it all by themselves."

"Well," agreed Granny, "it was just the two of them for awhile, but shortly after it became well-established and word got around, the womenfolk—and a few gentle men— began appearing to offer their services in whatever way was needed. Acts of unconditional goodness were performed out of the kindness of their hearts. Simple, yet beautiful acts. Some would even stop by just to plant a few flowers with the idea of adding a personal part of themselves to the grounds—they'd do nice little things like that. One trio of ladies lugged in a heavy birdbath and positioned it in line with one of the windows so it could be viewed from inside; a young man put homemade birdhouses on some of the trees. You just never knew. It was always such a pleasant and completely unexpected surprise to come upon new gifts of gratitude folks left. Oh, yes," she emphasized with increasing pleasure, "by that time those early detractors were up against a lot more women defenders of the place than just Sally and the Mother. A lot more!"

The Child fell into a giggling fit.

Taken aback, the old woman asked, "That's funny?"

"Kinda," Little Self readily admitted with a widening smile. "It's sorta funny because I pictured an army of women standing guard in a line in front of the abbey!"

"Oh, tsk, tsk, Child. You're way too visual. More to the point, you're far too imaginative! It never got like that. You've been watching too many Xena shows!"

"Xena. She's pretty cool, but fooled you . . . I don't watch that program."

"Doesn't matter. Same principle applies. You're far too imaginative. You can't let that imagination stretch into exaggerations. Gotta watch that. Gotta watch that real close or, before you know it, it'll get away from you. Keep to the facts, Little Self, keep to the facts."

"I know!" squealed the Child. "I know, but it's still fun imagining things. Imagination is fun! It's what inventions are made of," she cleverly slipped in.

The Crone shook her head. "Do you have an answer for everything?"

"Nope, that's why I have lots more questions for you.

What about the Changes?" came the next question before a breath was taken between sentences. "Obviously the Mother's place is still standing or I wouldn't be in it right now. It survived the Changes . . . and I guess the Mother and Sally came through them okay too."

The Crone rolled her eyes to the ceiling. "Has it ever occurred to you that it might do your young body good to come up for air between your churning thoughts," she suggested.

"Nuh-uh. I have lots and lots of air," Little Self informed. "So? What about the Changes?"

"All right, all right, we can get into those if you want," the old woman conceded. "Clearly, as you've so astutely noted, this place survived and so did its occupants, but don't forget," she said, tapping the side of her head, "that we're dealing with reality here—we're dealing with the reality of probabilities. The Mother has yet to experience the time for those changes and things may turn out a bit differently than you see here. Do you understand what I'm saying?"

"Sure I do. The way this place is today may not be exactly how it will turn out to be when the Mother catches up with this time—depending, of course, if the probabilities all manifest in the exact same way or not. Sure I get what you're saying, but mostly, things will be okay for them?"

Grandma was somewhat amused over the Child's exceptional mind. Inwardly she smiled while outwardly giving no indication of her satisfaction. "Generally it looks that way. We'll see how things end up when and if the Mother actually reaches the age of ninety-four.

"Anyway," the Crone continued, "for many years it was complete pandemonium in various places around the world. Those people who were skeptical of the predictions and laughed at those who were making preparations were completely caught off guard with nothing of their own to rely on. They were literally in shock and total bewilderment after being left with nothing to survive with. As you can imagine, they were the ones who were worst off.

"Those who'd prepared with solar energy as their alternative source of power weren't much better off, due to the many long months without sunlight. Those who planned with wind-powered generators fared better. And those who had stored massive amounts of gasoline and oil for their generators did the best because they ended up only running their generators for short periods of time each day for water; their energy availability was extended for months and months—for as long as it was needed.

"The power grid worldwide was down for several years. Nothing electronic worked. Cities were crippled and devastated by looters. People's humanness turned into a wild primitiveness based on the survival of self. Most all forms of rationale, courtesy, and camaraderie blew away on the sweeping Winds of Change. Roaming groups of ill-prepared and desperate people raided the vacated dwellings they came across. No vehicles worked. No gasoline was to be had anywhere. Stores were ransacked and gutted of their contents. There weren't enough military forces to be everywhere at once; in fact, the military forces weren't much in evidence for quite some time. It was night for a long time and hospitals weren't of much use."

"Why, Granny? Why weren't they of much use? Where were the military people?"

"Well, Dear, think about it. All the hospital and military personnel were too busy tending to the welfare of their own families, so attending to one's job or profession was not the priority for a long time; self-preservation was. Organizations like the Red Cross weren't effective. Not only were there not enough supplies to hand out to people, there were no workers to do the job because they were all intent on caring for their own immediate family needs. Everything broke down. All the emergency services weren't effectively in place because no one was manning them. Everyone's priority was attending to their own home and family.

"Imagine a major earthquake happening in your city or a volcano blowing and sending rivers of lava flow through the main streets of towns and covering entire residential subdivisions. Would you still feel like going to work, or attending to getting your family to safety? Home and family were the priorities people had. Going off to work at the Red Cross or Emergency Services jobs were not priorities, at least not until things settled down. See what I mean?"

The youngster nodded.

"And imagine how this would be if the disasters were widespread around the world in conjunction with the power grid being out everywhere. This is what I'm talking about when I refer to no one attending to the regular emergency services we think about when such events happen. This includes hospital and military elements as well.

"Eventually, little by little after many months of confusion, some order returned. Nobody recouped all their losses due to the widespread devastation that financially overwhelmed the insurance companies. The floor fell out of the Stock Exchange and everyone was penniless for quite a long time. As the years passed, the various elements of life sorted themselves out and were restored to near normalcy . . ."

The Child squinted in question, "Near normalcy?"

"Why, yes. Nothing could be exactly how it was. The shape of the landscape had dramatically altered. Many former cities were gone—wiped away—and new ones slowly sprung up. It took years of rebuilding and it began with folks volunteering and bartering before the monetary system returned. New roads had to be blazed. Bridges spanning large waterways were down and many dams failed. Familiar lakes disappeared and new ones formed elsewhere. There was much to do everywhere and it was the goodness in people's hearts that prevailed in the end."

The little one thoughtfully glanced about her. "How was it that this place remained untouched with so much being destroyed elsewhere? Did it suffer damage?" the Child asked, while scrutinizing the walls and ceilings for signs of structural damage.

"I never meant to imply that all buildings were destroyed. Many, many of them came through with little or no damage." The Crone's eyes scanned the room. "Oh, there were some structural effects felt here, but nothing we couldn't repair. The ground shifted a bit when the trembling first started. We were fortunate that we weren't nearer the epicenters."

"Epicenters? There were more than one around here?"

"Oh, my, yes! This place rumbled like thunder for days on end and we'd feel the tremors ripple across the floor in waves of energy. It was quite unnerving, never knowing if this was going to be the one to bring the cabin tumbling down around us. They weren't all the same, Little Self. Sometimes the earthquakes were just mild rumbles passing beneath the place and other times, other times they came as deafening cracks of thunder, then the earth violently shuddered for several minutes. You never knew," she said in recall, "you never knew until it happened."

The Child's eyes grew wider. "It sounds like those were scary times, like always living on pins and needles from the constant state of unpredictability."

The elder gave a wry smile. "Well, I couldn't say that we weren't frightened at times. There was a long while when we slept fully clothed because we never knew when we'd have to dash outside. Historically, this was never viewed as 'earthquake country' and then to experience them at increasing intervals forced us to become experienced with them. We had no choice but to learn and learn quickly how to react."

"How did the wildlife fare?"

"They managed just like the rest of us. I recall one of the first times the ground moved and it was one of those types that came like a thunder crack. The deer were out by the birdbath feeding and Sally and I were sitting right here watching them. When the crack came and the ground rumbled and shook, the deer all darted at once and disappeared. They moved so fast that it seemed as though they vanished into thin air in an instant. It was quite a sight, quite an experience.

"On the whole, the wildlife was thrown into confusion for a time because their natural instincts—their sense of the earth's magnetic field was constantly being disturbed. Eventually they grew accustomed to the routine disturbances and, I thought, adjusted quite well. The animals in the cities didn't fair as well though, so many of them were forced to fend for themselves, some died, some were rescued, and the rest became feral."

"Were there a lot of lives lost? People's lives?"

"Oh, yes, from all sorts of causes. There was a high rate of death from suicides because so many people thought the end of the world had come and there wasn't going to be any reason to go on living. Many thought that Armageddon was upon them, others waited for weeks as they gathered together in various groups to be ascended into heaven, or picked up by a mass rescue effort by hovering spaceships. None of those things happened. It was terrible, just terrible the way people lost their sense of rationale with crazy ideas. Yet, in the end, everything sorted itself out, and well . . . here we are today, you and I sitting together in a little cottage that'd seen it all.

"Remember, Little Self, I told you that, right now, you have all those memories in your head because you're here with me. We don't have to spend our time talking about the past, you know."

"Yes, I remember what you said, but I just had a couple of questions that I was curious about and wanted to hear the answers from you. The abbey especially was one of those things I was most interested in hearing about." Then the Child grinned. "That's the errand Sally's on, isn't it?"

The Crone returned the smile. "Yes, she likes to putter around the grounds and keep it neat and orderly, check to make sure nobody's been up to mischief again. Personally, I'd love to go up and tend to its flower gardens but, since I can't, she goes up there at least once a week to care for the flowers and keep the wild growth from encroaching. I go with her once in awhile but most times my presence causes a distraction for those visiting the sanctuary. That's the reason I need to stay away."

"That's too bad," said the Child with a frown.

"Why's that too bad? The place isn't for me, it's for all those seeking some spiritual quietude. If I'm there, people want to talk with me instead of gaining the serenity they went there for. That doesn't hurt my feelings—knowing I need to stay away. When the idea for the Magdalene Abbey first came to me I always understood that it wasn't for me personally, that I was only to build it for others. My goodness, Dear, I don't need to be there for it to fulfill its purpose."

"I see what you mean. Sorta like the difference between the Message and the Messenger," said the youngster before becoming pensive.

Chapter Six

The elder waited for the little one to voice her thoughts. The intense energy the small mind was putting out was palatable. The wise one waited with patience.

"Ummm, Granny?"

"Ehh?"

When the questions came, they came one after the other like a string of beads. "About those bad times . . . if people were left penniless, how'd they pay their bills? Make their house and car payments? And credit cards, what'd they do about all their plastic debts? How'd they buy food and clothing and . . ."

The old woman's head tilted toward the Child. "Whoa, there. Think, my dear. Isn't it obvious?"

The girl frowned. Then her eyes lit up. "There were no bills coming in anymore! There were no people in office buildings to send them. All the computers were crashed. Records vanished!"

Grandma clapped her hands. "Yes! Squatters moved into the houses people vacated in their exodus away from disaster areas. Later on, only those people who thought to protect and save their legal papers—their deeds and such to prove ownership—kept their properties. All banks and credit card companies folded because records were deleted. The entire financial aspect of society crashed along with their computers and the extended absence of electricity.

"Oh, Little Self, it was something to see! Financially, it was like wiping the slate clean for everyone. It wasn't like the great stock market crash when just the investors lost everything—this time everyone was left with only what they had in their pockets! Or the cash they'd shoved under their mattresses or buried in the yard! But," she brightened, "there was balance to that because people's debts were erased too! Everyone, and I mean everyone, was in the same boat. For a long time there were no more Haves and Have Nots, at least not financially, at least like it was before. Those who could be considered as being the Haves were those who'd planned well ahead with foresight and had stores of food and supplies and some cash reserve set aside. Do you see what I'm saying?"

The Child's braids bobbed while the Crone continued.

"So then, the entire societal criteria for perceiving wealth shifted. It shifted from actual money . . . to goods. And the 'goods' I'm talking about were not Mercedes, Ming vases, and ruby necklaces either; they were the simple things like supplies of those everyday medicines people routinely keep in their bathroom cabinets, toilet paper, canned food, gasoline, fresh eggs, and so on.

"You asked about how folks paid their bills, well, those bills became nonexistent. They were one of the first things to go when the economic element of society became leveled to a flat-line and there was no more financial pulse left to pick up on or give CPR to."

The Child smiled. "Maybe some things about the Changes weren't so bad if it got rid of the Haves and Have Nots," she expressed. "I was sure there'd be some good things that'd come from them. Oh, look!" she suddenly exclaimed, pointing toward the window, "the deer are leaving. Do you think we could go outside for awhile? I mean, since the twilight is holding while we're together like this, maybe we could go for a little walk." Then her countenance turned to one of concern, "Or are you tired?"

"Tired!" quipped the old one with a tone heavily weighted with indignance. "Do I look like I need to retire for the night or in need of a nap?"

The Child snickered. "Nooo."

"Okay then," she said before shifting into a more serious mode. "Well, Little Self, if we left this cottage it would no longer be twilight, would it? Perhaps we could attempt to leave the house, but we couldn't go as far as stepping outside that garden gate together."

The youngster knew what that meant. It meant that their meeting would be abruptly concluded and the Child would be transported back in her own time once again.

"I changed my mind," smiled the little one. "I wouldn't want to disturb that raccoon family on the porch."

"I think that's a good idea, I wouldn't want to do that either," the elder replied as she stood. "Come into the kitchen and see if you'd like to help me with a little project I'd planned on starting tonight."

"A project? I love working on projects. What is it . . . what is it?" she eagerly asked, following close behind the lacy hem of the grandma's long skirt.

"Oh, you'll see. Get in that cupboard," she said, pointing to the pantry, "and bring the nutmeg, cinnamon, and whole cloves over to the table while I get the plates and oranges."

"Pomanders!" Little Self squealed. "We're going to make autumn pomanders, aren't we. The Mother makes those, too."

"Uh-huh, that's exactly what we're going to do. Is that an okay project for us to busy ourselves with?"

"Oh, yes, I love making those. I love the smell of them. Do you also have some ribbon?"

The old woman rummaged in a drawer and then winked as she held up colorful satin skeins of orange and maroon ribbon. "Autumn colors. Chrysanthemum colors."

Chapter Seven

"Oh Granny, don't you just love fall?" Realizing what she'd said, the Child caught herself and corrected her comment. "Well, silly me, of course you love fall . . . we always did, didn't we?" Then she grinned, "All three of us."

"Mmmm, that's a fact. Always," she grinned back with a mutter under her breath. "You are one impish child."

The girl's eyes playfully sparkled as they locked on the grandma's. "I know," she proudly admitted. "That's my job."

The two busied themselves arranging all the makin's for the fragrant pomanders. The large bowl of oranges was placed in the center of the table and the spices were lined up in a row along with the ribbon and scissors.

The Child skeptically eyed the ingredients. "Ummm. Granny?"

"Yes?"

"Where's the orris root? Don't you still use orris root as a preservative when you make these?"

The elder tilted her head back to peer through her wire granny glasses perched at the end of her nose. "Well, I'll be!" she exclaimed. "You're right. Would you go get it from the spice cupboard?"

"Yep!" the Child squeaked. "Be right back."

Grandma shook her head and sighed. "I must be getting old and senile to forget the orris root. Never forgot an ingredient in my life. This is a first."

Setting the retrieved jar on the table, the Child soothed, "Oh, Granny, you would've remembered just as soon as we started working. I can't imagine you ever getting forgetful, much less senile. Old age never means senility, you know."

"I know that, but there's no denying that I am getting up there," she said while taking an orange in one hand and reaching for the cloves with the other. "I've been blessed throughout all these years. I'm still quite spry of body, and the mind, thank the Goddess above, remains well intact. I still read just as much as I used to and manage to get out in those woods nearly every single day." She leaned forward and flashed a conspiratory wink, "Sometimes I still get out there in the middle of the night—just like the Mother does."

Little Self grinned.

"And my gardening keeps me busy. Oh, yes, that gardening certainly keeps this old woman busy. Did you happen to notice how beautiful the Boston ivy is on the place?"

The Child's eyes grew wide. "Yes! Back in my time the Mother is still wondering if she'll be able to grow it. When she was a little girl it grew all over the house we grew up in and she's been wanting very much to try to grow it on her cabin. She's not so sure it'll grow at this elevation and has put off trying it." Little Self gave the old one a knowing grin then. "I guess she eventually goes ahead and tries it, huh, Granny."

"Huh. You got that right. It worked, didn't it?"

"I'll say it worked, it's beautiful. She's going to be so happy to know that it'll work!"

Hearing that last, Granny raised a brow. "And just how is she going to hear about that?"

The impish grin returned. "I'll put a bug in her ear."

"When? When will you do that?"

"When I get back, get back to my time—her time—after I leave here."

"Oh," came the clipped reply.

The Child sprinkled equal amounts of the nutmeg, orris root, and cinnamon together into a large bowl. While she thoroughly stirred the ingredients, mixing them well, she snuck surreptitious looks at the busy woman across from her.

The wise Crone, knowing the Child held an urgent question within her, was humming while sticking the cloves into the orange skin. She was busy making a quartered pattern that left spacings for the ribbon to be wrapped around and then tied off into a loop at the top for hanging. The old one held a secret. This the Child sensed and was antsy to discover.

Little Self cleared her throat. "Ahemm. Granny?"

"Mmmm, child?"

"I said something wrong, didn't I? About putting that bug in the Mother's ear."

"Wrong?"

The Child nodded.

The old one shrugged.

"Yes, I do know I said something wrong, but I can't seem to figure out exactly what it was."

Without looking up from her work, the elder softly inquired. "Are you quite sure you said something wrong?"

"I'm sure."

"Well then, perhaps you'd better think harder on it and see if you can't discover what it was."

Little Self grabbed an orange and began sticking cloves into it. She was deep in thought. The deeper she thought, the more her mouth scrunched up with the effort and the more force was used to push in the cloves.

The old one's heart smiled to see the youngster's mental intensity.

Though the Child continued to diligently work, she slid her gaze up to lock on the old one's. "Is this supposed to be some kind of big secret or something?"

"Secret?" the Crone repeated. "There are no secrets to reality, Little Self. There are no secrets, big or little. You know that—only those yet unrealized elements of it. Those elements are neither secrets nor hidden facets, only natural aspects that the human mind has yet to discover. They're there like that unseen beetle beneath the seen rock."

"Well, yes, I know that, Granny," she sullenly replied looking back down at her work, "I need to think on this some more."

Silence.

The elder waited while the youngster's nimble fingers furiously jammed a dozen or more cloves into the orange.

Then the small hands stopped.

Little Self looked into the other's expectant eyes. "I won't be able to put a bug about the ivy into the Mother's ear when I get back because I'll be back in her time and not have any memories in my mind about our time here together because our time together was in the future."

A tender smile curled up the old one's lips. "See there? That wasn't so hard, was it?"

The Child wasn't sure she liked what she'd just discovered. Disappointed, she sputtered, "But that means that I won't be able to look at all those memories of what happened between 1999 and 2040 when I get back to the Mother's time. I won't be able to convey anything about them to her."

The old woman calmly said, "That's right, you won't, Child."

The little one was quiet as she thought more on that.

Grandma tilted her head then. "Does that bother you, Little Self? Does it upset you that you won't remember the memories you now hold in your mind?"

"No," she reticently admitted, " I guess not because when I get back to the Mother's time they won't be memories anyway, they'll be our future—our probable future." The little one paused before continuing. "It won't matter because, somewhere in my being, I'll have an inner knowing that the Mother will be okay. That'll be good enough for me. All the specifics won't matter as long as I know that she'll survive."

The old one raised a brow in unspoken question.

The Child caught the intent. "Well yes, I know about the probability thing that can alter outcomes but, generally, I'll have the feeling that things will work out . . . one way or another. And, who knows," she added with a gleam in her eye, "maybe I'll even have some inkling about that Boston ivy after all."

"Who knows?" echoed the elder giving an encouraging smile. "This is all so new, Little Self. Who is to say what the true extent of residual feelings you may retain from this meeting will turn out to be? As far as I know, it's never been done before. Experimental ventures, even those into the vast potentialities of Time, blaze new trails and break through old barriers once thought to be formidably impenetrable. Mmm? We learn marvelous new and exciting truths from them—new beautiful and amazingly spectacular aspects to reality—and from these we intellectually grow and mature in the wisdom we've gained. So, I suppose, even as we sit here making autumn pomanders, we'll just have to be patient—wait and see what sort of feelings and subtle knowings you do retain after returning to your own time."

The Child smiled, then frowned. "Granny?"

"Mmmm, Dear?"

"I don't want to forget about our time together. I don't think that'd be right," she declared with a semi-pout. "It wouldn't be fair. I mean, after all, what would be the point of our meeting if I had no memory of ever doing it once I got back?"

"Right? Fair?" The old woman cocked her silvery head. "Isn't the meeting the whole point? Isn't the whole point being that the Child and the Crone aspects within one woman's feminine consciousness managed to actualize a physical face-to-face meeting and converse? Converse and interact just like two separate individuals? Ohh, Little Self," she gently cautioned like a deeply concerned teacher, "don't lose sight of what's been accomplished here, Honey . . . what's been *given*.

"As sure as I know that your name is Little Self, I'm also just as sure that this meeting was a most precious gift from the loving heart of Mother Sophia herself. Look at what our gift has already entailed, Child. We've already hugged one another, had fun working on craft projects together, and touched each other's hearts so deeply that we've each had to wipe tears from our eyes. All of those things were gifts within the gift She gave us. To expect more from it is placing yourself in Expectation, it's wanting more for yourself out of it instead of fully appreciating the accomplishment of the feat itself and recognizing what a magnificent gift we've been given."

Hanging her head, the Child whispered, "Then should I be ashamed for wanting to recall everything after I return to the Mother's time? That's how you make it sound." She suddenly raised her head and proudly looked straight into the Crone's eyes. "Because, if I should, I don't."

"You don't?"

"Nope. Not a twinge."

"Do you know why you don't feel any twinge of guilt over that?"

Twin braids swung from side to side as the Child shook her head. "No, I just don't, that's all. Do you know why?"

The old one slowly nodded.

"Do I have to guess? Are you going to make me figure it out for myself?" asked the Child.

"I don't think we came together this day to play guessing games, Little Self. What would be the purpose of that? Seems to me that that'd only be a waste of precious time, a waste of an invaluable experience, a waste of the very special gift we were given. You didn't give me time to answer your question. You're too impatient for answers.

"Of course, I'm going to tell you. You feel no sense of shame or guilt for wanting to recall our time together and the things you've learned here after you return to your own time because your heart is pure."

The Child frowned at that. It wasn't the answer she expected. She didn't get it.

"You see? You see your immediate response?" the old one continued. "That response of puzzlement proves what I just said. Those with pure hearts don't even realize they have pure hearts because it's so natural and inherent in them. But I know," the Crone cooed. "I know that your heart is pure and it's the very reason you feel no shame over wanting to recall these events. You simply wanting to be able to help guide the Mother through the worst of the Changes when they begin happening is evidence of that. But," she reminded, raising a finger in the air, "you're forgetting that that's why I'm here in the Mother's consciousness. That subtle inner guidance of the Mother's comes from my end—my Crone aspect of her consciousness. And I'm certainly not going to keep her in the dark when things start getting sticky. She'll have some of that Knowing . . . just like always before."

The Child had finished poking all her cloves into the orange skin and rolled the prickly ball around in the spicy blend of powder. "So . . . is it a . . . a 'my job/your job' kind of thing?"

The elder's expression softened. "Oh no, no, not really. It's more like that just seems to be the way of it. You handled her childhood griefs and I naturally take care of guiding her ongoing steps because I'm more aware of the future.

"It's the togetherness, the cooperative efforts of both of us working to guide the Mother's present-day footpath through life. It takes us both, Little Self. It takes us both." She rolled her own orange in the mixture and, while doing so, eyed the youngster. "Perhaps there will be some memories—strong inklings—retained when you return to your time. Who is to say for sure? This is the first time this has happened and we'll have to wait to see how it all turns out when all is said and done."

"Yeah," the Child happily smiled back, "who's to say? Maybe I'll even remember *all* of it!"

The old one gave a look of feigned admonishment. "Oh, dear, now look who's the optimist!"

The Child's face scrunched in reaction. "Well, maybe that was a bit much to expect, maybe I'll just remember *most* of it."

The elder's expression didn't alter.

The Child backed off. "Maybe *some* of it."

The expression remained.

"Well, maybe a *teeny* bit."

And the Crone smiled as each of them finished coating their oranges and reached for another to work on.

A silence, thick with warm camaraderie, hovered over

the two while they busied themselves like Santa's elves on Christmas eve, each content in the warm and loving companionship that had quickly developed between them.

Suddenly, like an opened Jack-in-the-box, the Child abruptly popped up out of her chair and hopped about the table in animated excitement. She spun around like a gyroscope.

Granny nearly jumped out of her chair. "Oh! Oh, my! Oh, dear!" she startled, fluttering her hand to her chest. "My goodness, Child, you can't do things like that around old people! You almost gave me a heart attack. What in the world's got into you?"

"Granny!" the gyroscope sputtered. "I just figured it out! I just now figured it out!"

"Pray tell. What?" the old woman quickly asked while placing both hands on the bowl of powder to keep it from tipping. "Get it out, girl! Get it out before you start knocking things over!"

The Child paced with unrestrained energy. "It's not an issue of job at all! It's about beingness! I'm the Child Within and you're the Crone Within."

Now it was the old one's turn to scrunch up her face. "Well, you knew that! For heaven's sake, Child, you knew that! Why act as though you didn't, for heaven's sake?"

"Because I hadn't made the connection to the Crone aspect being what it was . . . is! I'm the Child aspect in *every* woman's consciousness. Right?"

"Right."

"But you're the Crone aspect of every woman's consciousness, the elder with wisdom—the Higher Self aspect of every woman's consciousness!" The Child planted herself down in the chair, balled up a small fist and pounded her knee. "I can't believe I hadn't made that connection before this!"

"Oh, stop berating yourself," came the friendly chastising reply from across the table. "Tsk-tsk. My goodness, you'd think you just committed some terrible spiritual crime the way you're acting."

"But Granny!" spat the Child as she slapped her palms down hard on the table.

The bowls rattled.

Grandma reached for them as the youngster rambled on. "It's so, so . . . well, so obvious! It's so obvious that every woman's Crone aspect is really her own Higher Self!"

"Oh, really! Apparently not!" replied the old woman, while rearranging the table items. "It's apparently not so obvious, Little Self, not when so many women in the world think they need psychics to tell them what to do or when so many women automatically misinterpret their own Higher Self—their Crone aspect—as being some separate Grand Poobah or Indian Chief spirit guide! Or God. Or some Goddess talking to them. Or the voice of the Virgin Mary. Oh no," she sighed, "it's not obvious at all. Women need to get control of their lives back by going Within—to their own elder Within who holds their own inherent wisdom and can best guide their footfalls, because it's that elder who knows all the private and personal elements about that woman's purpose that no one else does . . . or can know.

"Instead, women run themselves ragged racing hither and yon to the ends of the earth seeking those Without and end up spinning their wheels in an endless effort to get accurate, personal information. They're always searching for that special mysterious or high and mighty someone who will point them in the right direction, looking for specific answers from those who can only offer fad philosophies and worn out clichés, and reaching for diamonds of wisdom that turn out to be worthless imitations."

The Child made a sad face and frowned. "The Crone within every woman is ignored then, isn't it, Granny?"

"On the whole, yes, I'd say it was. I think that's a valid statement," she replied while rolling another clove-filled orange around in the spice mixture. "The concept of the Crone aspect of a woman's consciousness isn't myth; that wise old Crone is each woman's true Higher Self and is always there giving precious insights and inspiration. But," she sighed, "they don't listen."

"I'm sorry," the young one soothed. "I'm sorry it's that way."

"Ahh, well."

Then the corners of Little Self's mouth tipped up to form an impish smile. "She's also a muse," she whispered. "The Crone, I mean. She's also a muse, isn't she."

Likewise, one corner of the old one's mouth rose as she eyed the youngster sitting across the table. "In a way she is, in a way, because she inspires epiphanies and valuable philosophical ideologies to the Mother aspect. The Crone within every woman is like the old Wise Woman of the village who everyone highly respected and went to for guidance."

"And she's always there, isn't she, Granny. She's always available and waiting for the women to come to her but . . . but they don't because they don't realize she's so accessible to them."

"That's right."

"That's not right. I mean, that's a shame. Why do people always make something hard when it's really so easy and simple?"

"Shame or otherwise, Little Self, that seems to be how it is in the world. Women need to awake to the Old Wise One Within themselves—their feminine Higher Self. They need to wake up to the fact that they hold the answers to all their seeking right inside their own minds, their own precious consciousness." The Crone released a heavy sigh. "Ahhh, yesss, women need to learn to love and to trust themselves." She glanced out the window. "Uh-huh, that's what they need to do, all right."

No response was forthcoming from the younger one. None was necessary. It'd all been said . . . almost all.

The two continued to enjoy working together on their craft project while sharing such meaningful conversations. Several moments passed before the Child broke the silence.

"Is it different now? In your time, is it better?"

"For what? Better for what, Child? Are you asking if the women in my time have come to realizations about their Higher Self, their trined aspects?"

The Child sheepishly nodded, not sure if she truly wanted to hear the answer.

"Well, it's certainly better, I'll say that much about it. Many of them have come to their senses after seeing the futility of seeking their answers outside of themselves. At least they've come to understand that only a woman can hold the answers for a woman's search.

"In the old days—back in your time—women couldn't seem to differentiate between men's philosophy and women's wisdom. There'd always been such a vast difference, you know."

The Child nodded.

"Anyway," the elder said, "they'd hear about some new teacher or popular guru and rush off to glean what bits of sparkling wisdom they could from them—regardless of the gender of these absolute strangers. And that's where many of them made their big mistake. The women gave no consideration to the simple and basic fact that men's philosophy was very different from women's wisdom. Men's is linear, women's is circular. Men's is of the letter of the law, women's is of the conceptual spirit of it. Each outwardly is perceived and inwardly received in a different manner. Spiritually, men and woman have variant needs and, as such, have different naturally inherent methods of spiritual expression.

"But during the passing of time between your day and mine, women have learned that a woman needs woman's wisdom. Women have discovered that it was the missing element in their lives, that their hearts and souls had been silently yearning for, craving. Since then they've made a slow and subtle return to the ancient ideology of the village old Wise Woman and understand that only a woman can fully understand the problems and dilemmas of a woman. So then, when their specific quest was related to a person-alized life situation, they eventually discovered that the best source of that guiding wisdom was the Crone Within themselves—their own feminine Higher Self.

"Eventually, as time passed, the reality of this basic con-ceptual truism was understood by the men and it caught on as they began seeking out male spiritual teachers. So, the women conferred with a wise old woman or, most often, went within themselves to consult their own Crone aspect who, by the way, knew far more about the woman's per-sonal situation than anyone else ever could. This they learned."

"Of course, she knew more," emphasized the Child, "she knew everything about the woman's life, her purpose, and even what her future held. Of course, she knew all that because she was the Crone aspect of her very own con-sciousness!"

"See there? See what I mean?" the old one under-scored. "It all seems so obvious, so simple, to you and me, but for Ms. Everywoman out there it wasn't so clear and simple, was it? It took considerable time for them to come to the realization. It took a lot of time for the light to come on. Don't forget, Dear, women had been suppressed and held down by the hand of patriarchy for centuries."

"At least it happened, though," smiled the Child. "At least the women of my time finally saw that light and came into their own inner power."

The elder's silver, wispy brows went up. "That's one way to put it. Coming into their own power. I think I like that."

And the Child's smile widened with the unexpected compliment. "Thanks," she piped.

"Ohhh, don't thank me, Little Self. You come up with some good ones now and again—some really good ones. I've heard you. You and I make quite a team, you know."

Coming from the wise Crone, the comment sent a wave of warmth through the Child's heart. She felt it suddenly settle and glow within her small chest. "Yeah, we're a team, aren't we, Granny. You, the Mother, and me. We make quite a team all by ourselves and have managed to wriggle through some pretty rough stuff in the Mother's life."

"Yes, Child, we certainly have done that," the old woman agreed before falling into the weighted silence of deep contemplation.

Chapter Eight

As the youngster worked on her next orange she felt an inexplicable sense of uneasiness settle between them. "Granny?"

"Mmmm?"

"Is something wrong?"

The thin shoulders rose and fell in silent reply.

Little Self tilted her head. "Granny? What's up?"

"I feel I need to talk to you about something."

"What?"

"Well? I feel that I need to advise you to contain yourself better, Little Self. Have better control over your impetuosity."

The youngster's shoulders slumped. "Oh," she whispered, as eyes lowered in downcast guilt.

"Uh-huh. You know what I'm talking about, don't you?"

Without looking up, the small head slowly nodded.

"When you're back in your own time with the Mother you need to get a better hold on your exuberance. You can't let it pop out like you have in the past. You can't let it get away from you."

Now the Child's small shoulders hitched back up. "I try, Granny, I really do!"

"I know you do," Granny admitted, "but you need to try harder. You can't just pop out on the Mother when she's around people. Little Self," she kindly reminded, "that's not being fair to her."

"You're talking about that time when that special movie about the fairies came on television, aren't you."

"Yes, that time and also a few others that I can recall off the top of my head."

"Well, that time I really couldn't help it. I was so excited to watch it and the Mother's company was rude, Granny. They were all talking at once and I couldn't hear the program."

"You can't do that, Little Self. You cannot do that. You must restrain yourself from breaking through like that."

Like a bolt of lightning out of the blue, the youngster flashed bright and powerful in defense of herself. "I didn't! I didn't break through then! The Mother felt my excitement and then my impatience. She caught me. She stopped me. And then she made the compromise by talking with her company and keeping an eye on the program for me. Besides," she contrarily announced with a pout, "*Sally* likes it when I talk to her."

"But we're not talking about your conversations with *Sally*, are we? Mmmm? We're specifically talking about those instances when you break through the Mother's consciousness at inappropriate times. We're talking about your precocious and spontaneous behavior that you cannot allow yourself to give in to."

"But, Granny! Sometimes I just get so excited over things I can't help it!"

"You can," said the elder calmly. "You can help it and you must."

The Child again lowered her head. She studied her fingers. "Are you angry with me?"

"No, not angry. I'm just reminding you of your job and its perimeters. Neither of us can overstep those bounds. We both have our proper places within the feminine consciousness, Little Self. We cannot forget those places—either of us. That goes for me as well as for you."

"Yes, but you're the elder," she whispered while weaving her fingers together. "You're the wise one. You know better."

Granny's eyes widened in astonishment. "Tsk-tsk! Shame on you. Don't go pulling that innocent 'I'm just a kid so I don't know any better' ploy on me, Child. You do know better. You know as well as I do. You're just as in tune with the higher spiritual forces as I am. You're aware of the same rules as I am." The elder shook her head. "You can be a real piece of work sometimes, you know that? Little Self," she gravely cautioned, "don't use your knowledge as an excuse for inappropriate behavior. Don't ever do that. And especially, don't ever twist that knowledge to serve your own agenda."

"Sorry, Granny," the Child apologized. "I'm sorry I get so excited sometimes."

"I'm not asking for an apology and I don't want one. There's not a thing wrong with you getting so excited at times, that's an inherent element of our trined personality and, as I think you know, that's not at all what we're talking about here." The Crone's voice was soft and understanding. "What we're talking about is your need to keep a tight rein on that exuberance, Little Self. You do need to restrain it more than you have in the past. Restraint. That's what we're talking about. That's what this is all about."

"I'll try, Granny. I really will, I promise. But it's just so hard for me to do all the time. Sometimes my excitement just explodes before I even realize it was ready to go off. It just shoots outta me."

"That's impetuosity, Little Self. That's what we're talking about."

The youngster didn't reply.

Grandma smiled amusingly at the Child's attempt to rationalize her behavior. "Maybe it wouldn't be quite so hard to do if you'd just once—just once—stop to think about or visualize how your behavior of 'popping out' might embarrass the Mother aspect when you do it when other people are around her. Think how that makes her look."

The Child had what she thought was the perfect comeback. "You've popped out a time or two. I've seen you do it."

"But, Little Self," the Crone gently informed, "that's not the same. That's not the same at all. My presence didn't make her look like a child, did it?"

Silence.

"Did it?"

"No," came the reluctant reply.

"Didn't the verbal response I once popped out with end up being the exact advice the person she was talking to needed?" Without waiting for another admission from the Child, the elder continued. "And the other times I came to the fore were to hold her quick tongue and give silence as a response. Think about that. Whenever I've given silence as a response, who's to know that it was really the Mother's own Higher Self—her Crone Within—who made that non-verbal reply? Who was to know it was anyone other than the Mother herself? And the other times, the other times were when she required certain calming words coming from her mouth to effectively extricate herself from some of those potentially explosive situations she was finding herself drawn into. See the difference, Little Self? Do you see the difference?"

The youngster looked down at the orange she held and rolled it around in her hands. "I suppose so."

"You suppose so? Little Self, this is extremely important. You need to fully understand this."

The Child did understand. She'd understood all along.
"I didn't mean to say 'suppose so,' I meant, yes. I do see.
But . . . but it's just so hard when I get so excited about
something. Granny, sometimes I see something in a store
that really, really attracts me and I want to run over and
examine it. I've been pretty good about holding that urge
down, haven't I?"

"Yes, indeed you have and I'm sure no one more than
the Mother appreciates that effort you've made."

"I hope so because it sure does take a lot of effort."

The elder reached her hand across the table for the
Child's.

The Child reached back.

They touched.

"You're doing a fine job, Little Self. Don't take my
advice as being a verbal spanking. That's not what it's
meant to be."

"I know."

"You're a sweet, sweet child. The world would be a better place if more children were of as pure of heart as you
are. I hate telling you to curb your excitement because it's
like having to put a lid on happiness, but you and I are
aspects of the Mother and we must work within our spiritual bounds. Those bounds are there for a very special reason, they have purpose. They are the perimeters that keep
the trined aspects of a consciousness uniquely separate.
The Mother aspect is the only one allowed to live the
Present time frame as it's happening. We're here as support. We can only visit," she smiled then, "pop out into the
present only in emergency situations. That's important to
remember—very important. Always."

The Child's fingers squeezed the gnarled ones. "I know,

Granny. I know." She hesitated before asking her next question. "Was I wrong to pop out that evening in the Mother's stone cabin? Was I wrong to come out and talk to Sally?"

The elder squeezed the little hand back. "No, Dear, you did just right. Don't you think the way things were going that night designated an emergency situation?"

The Child nodded. "I thought so."

"And your judgement was commendable because your action served to verify many things for Sally and clarify all those strong inner promptings she'd been feeling. Revealing those past-life connections was important. They came at just the right time. Don't you see how validating that evening ended up being?"

"Yes. I thought it was important to say some things that needed to be said." She grinned, "I'm glad you're still with Sally, Granny. You make the bestest best friends. I really like her. I'm so glad she is where she was supposed to be—you know, in place. I'm glad it was her."

Grandma leaned her head toward the Child. "Can you keep a secret?"

The little one expectantly nodded.

"Me, too," whispered the elder with a magical twinkle spearing from her eye. "I'm glad too."

A big smile curled the corners of the Child's mouth. "Can you keep a secret?"

Grandma nodded.

The youngster whispered back. "*I know.*"

And they both laughed.

"Well!" said the old woman, perking up the mood, "shall we finish up this project?"

Little Self smiled and reached for the shiny, satin ribbon. "Which color do you want to start with?" she asked.

"Oh, I like to use them both on each ornament. That way they look more autumny, don't you think?"

The Child giggled. "I think that's a good idea. Would I look like a copycat if I did that too?"

"The answer's no, but the question is why would you care what it looked like?"

The Child sighed and pursed her lips. She gave the elder a narrow-eyed, sidelong look. "Are you always teaching something?"

"Oops. Does it show?"

"Does a mouse love peanut butter?"

The old woman gave the scissors a quick push. They slid across the light oak table. "Sorry about that 'teaching' thing. Must be an old habit. Maybe I need to watch that, huh?"

"Huh."

"Or maybe I don't," quipped the old one. "Being the Higher Self aspect, spiritual behavior is the most inherent part of my beingness. Teaching and bringing the elements of higher wisdom into subject matters is what I'm about. If I didn't take every opportunity to do that, then I'd be shirking my duty. Mmmm? Wouldn't that mean that I wasn't taking my job seriously?"

Knowing the question was also directed at her own behavior, the Child sighed, "I suppose," came the less than enthusiastic reply before the subject was changed.

Chapter Nine

While busy measuring the lengths of ribbon and snipping them off just right, the Child commented in an offhanded manner, "There's no birdsong in the cabin. I noticed that you don't have birds anymore. How come, Granny? How come you don't?"

"Now you're jumping to an assumed conclusion based on circumstantial evidence. I think you should've thought a bit deeper on that one before you came out with your question. Your mouth jumped ahead of your thinking process. Go on, think about it. I'll wait."

Little Self averted her eyes from the old woman's as she looked about the room, spying none of the birdcages she was used to seeing in the Mother's cottage, yet she heard raucous chirpings, cackles, and twitters from the covered front porch.

Her answer came quickly. "Now all of your birds are the wild ones. You do have birds, just not in cages inside the house anymore," she clarified. That fact brought related elements into the issue. "So, I'm wondering, why don't you have the little finches and parakeets in the house anymore? I'm wondering if it's got anything to do with events back when . . . well, I guess I'm asking . . . in the time following the Changes, are places like pet shops all gone now?"

The elder had been wrapping bright satin ribbon around one of the spiced oranges while listening to the Child's mental speculations. In response, she said, "Your hypothesis is close, but not precise. After the Changes people gained a raised level of respect and appreciation for all of life. They reconsidered the previous practice of capturing wildlife and taking it from the natural habitats and environments. The puppy mills disappeared and the professional breeders turned to putting their experience and energies into animal orphanages—wildlife adoption agencies. This originally came about after many geologic events loosed thousands upon thousands of stray pets into the city streets and countrysides. A great mass effort was expended to gather these poor creatures up and find them homes. Consequently, the glut of readily available, cost-free animals ran the pet shops right out of business and, after awhile, the free 'pounds' or animal adoption centers became more the way of life.

"The old practice of harvesting tropical fish from the oceans and reefs and wild birds from the rain forests soon followed suit. People became of a mind that tended toward 'naturalness' when it came to the animals' natural environment, after realizing that those species had a purpose in the overall health of the planet—the interconnected interdependence between flora and fauna. The people came to understand that taking these precious species from the tropical forests and oceans disturbed the fine balance of nature. Ergo, no little finches in cages and no fish in household aquariums, except for educational centers such as national and state aquariums and natural history observatories where every effort is made to maintain the natural habitat of each species.

"Oh yes, Little Self, we still have plenty of birds and birdsong around here. The difference between Then and

Now is that now it's just due to 'natural' occurrence instead of forced through capture and containment."

"That was beautiful," the Child sighed. "To think there'll be no more puppy mills really makes me happy. Remember Sally's Yorkie, Baby? And the awful condition she was in when Sally received her as a gift? That poor little dog had been in a breeder's cage for a year and a half and," Little Self emphasized by making an equally awful face, "her backside was covered with worms! No wonder Baby became so attached to Sally after she'd taken her to the vets and got her all cleaned up. What a pitiful way things sometimes were back then . . . back in my own time, I mean. I'm real happy to hear that that sort of thing will, someday, be a thing of the past. I'm happy to know that people will finally grow to respect the life of all life and make changes in behavior that reflects that respect." The Child grinned wide. "Yeah, I like that a lot," she said, while tying off her ribbon and then making a small loop at the top to create a hanger for the fragrant pomander.

"There! One done," she proudly exclaimed holding it up. "Are we making these for the cottage or for gifts?"

"Gifts. I'd like to be able to tell you that you could take that one home, but under the circumstances . . ."

" . . . under the circumstances," the little one knowingly finished, "it wouldn't arrive back with me. I can't take anything back that I didn't come with. That much I know to be true about this whole visit."

"You're probably right about that," offered the elder.

"Probably?"

"Well, Little Self, as far as I know, this is the first time this type of meeting has been managed, much less even attempted. Conceptually, I don't believe it's ever been done before. We're assuming that you wouldn't be able to take anything back with you that you didn't arrive here with. Who knows? Although I tend to agree with your thoughts on it. It seems reasonable that you couldn't, don't you think?"

"I suppose so," the little one softly groaned with heavy disappointment. "But wouldn't it be great if I could take something back with me?"

"Would it? You think so?"

"Oh, yes! After all," she reasoned, "I brought something here. I brought a basket and my dolly."

The Crone eyed the younger. "And just what would you consider this 'great' object being?"

"Ohhh, gosh Granny, I dunno. I think I'd have to give that some pretty deep thought because it'd have to be a really, really super special object," she decided as she reached for a new length of ribbon.

"I suppose you're right about that. I suppose it would have to be something really special."

And the two were silent then as the elder allowed the Child to think hard on what "special" object she'd choose to take back to the past with her.

Chapter Ten

The old woman smiled to herself as she sensed the intensity of the other's mind working.

Finally the Child asked a question without looking up from her work. "Granny?"

"Yes, Dear?"

"Ummm."

"Ummm?"

"The Mother . . . the Mother keeps a journal. She writes in it every single night. Is that, ummm, is that something she keeps doing in her future?"

"She never stopped. Oh, there were times when she skipped a few days; those were times when she got tired of writing about the same old things all the time—those days on end when she and Sally were caregivers and all the days were just like the day before—nothing different to write about. But then she'd go back, fill them in, and continue on where she'd left off. It became such a habitually ingrained part of her day that she automatically kept doing that through to her future." Then Granny suspiciously eyed the Child. "What you're really asking me is if *I* keep a journal. Hmmm? Isn't that it?"

The little one's head slowly bobbed in confirmation.

"Uh-huh. I thought so. Why, yes, Child, I do. I never stopped recording my days." Then the elder's dancing eyes widened. "Why, Little Self! Is *that* what you'd choose to take back with you?"

Sheepishly, the Child nodded. "But I guess that'd be wrong, huh? That'd be too personal and . . ."

"That'd be like taking a written record of the future back to the past! Ohhh, Little Self, tsk-tsk, that just wouldn't be allowed. Oh, no, that just would not be allowed. That'd never do."

The Child's shoulders fell. "Yeah, I figured you'd say that."

"Well it isn't just me, you know. My good gracious, it isn't just me! The high Spiritual Ones would never condone such a thing. The perimeters, remember?

"Besides," she tried to soften, "the writing on the pages would probably just disappear anyway."

Bemoaning her situation, the Child grumbled, "*Remember* the perimeters?" She repeated wtih a sigh, "how can I forget? Those are always in my way, at least it seems like they always are."

The wise Crone shot the Child a semi-chastising glance. "In your way? Oh, Little Self, you can't truly mean that," she softly replied, "we are bound by right action and the spiritual law of who we are and how we must work within the framework of our natural beingness, our purpose. We must never entertain an alternate view of those rules being anything other than the high guidelines they inherently are. Don't we hope that all those living in the physical behave in a spiritual manner?"

The Child nodded in firm agreement.

"So then, would we ourselves desire anything less—or more—than that? Would we ourselves be so arrogant to think our own behavior could ever be stretched to reach outside that spiritual law? Oh nooo, I don't think so. We uphold the spiritual law and work within its bounds, else chaos results.

"As the Mother's Child Within you have quite naturally taken on her childhood griefs and continue to absorb much of her ongoing heartaches whenever they occur in her life. You're the 'emotion buffer' and, at the same time, help to preserve her wonderful, wonderful childlike attributes. I, as the Mother's Crone Within, aid in guiding her footsteps along the destined trail she came to walk and instill needed insights and bits of so-called 'visionary' ideas into her thought process. Those are our jobs, Little Self. We're the support team of her consciousness, nothing more and certainly nothing less than that."

The Child listened well as she concentrated on her active hands that were busy wrapping maroon ribbon about the powdery orange. "Support team," she whispered in echo. "We're the natural aspects of her consciousness— we're the keepers of her soul."

The old woman let that profound thought set awhile in her mind before she responded. "Yes. Yes, indeed that's what we are. And what is it that you're getting at . . . precisely?"

"Keepers of the Soul," the Child said without looking up from her work, "that's what she was going to call the book about our meeting. Earlier you said that she titled it something else that I thought sounded weird. Why didn't she use the original title? I liked it. I liked it because it was so perfect. We are the keepers of her soul—her consciousness."

"All right, let's look at this. Originally, as you know, the Mother didn't just come up with the idea to do the book. It didn't just pop into her mind one day to do it. The concept never came into her mind until, one night, while deep in quantum meditation, she journeyed to the future and saw you out there," she informed, pointing in the direction of the hill that Little Self had previously rested upon with her doll and basket of sage.

"In her quantum state she was actually consciously—virtually—present when you began your journey here. Each consecutive meditative experience she had thereafter brought her into the next sequential scene of the same event. It was like going into meditation and picking up where the action left off where the previous one ended."

"Like watching a soap opera every day," compared the perceptive Child.

"Something very much like that. But then, certain ongoing events in her daily life became, well . . . stressors that . . ."

"The financial and caregiving elements," interjected the young one. "I know because they're going on right now—back in my time."

"Yes. Those among others, and she wasn't able to get into that deeper level of her meditations for some time after that to continue the sequential journey that she'd previously begun. She got as far as witnessing you come through the garden gate out there and then . . . nothing more . . . nothing more happened due to the daily pressures and work that'd been occupying her consciousness."

Little Self was confused. Her expression made that clear. "So how'd she end up doing the book then?"

"The idea for it kept nagging her and wouldn't let go, it just would not go away. That's when she went back and forth about doing it as a book. She desperately wanted to do it because she knew it was so important for the women of the world to understand the true nature of their consciousness, yet two related aspects of the idea continued to stay her hand."

The Child perked up. "I think I know what those were! Let me guess. She was leery of readership reaction to something so conceptually 'out there'—she didn't think they'd understand, and also, the fact that she couldn't write about something she never actually completed experiencing."

"That's right. That's exactly right."

"So? So, what happened to change those?"

The Crone's eyes twinkled then. "So she thought about all those very, very special readers of hers who would understand the concept of the Feminine Consciousness and it was her thoughts of them, Little Self. They did it. They were the ones who ended up reinforcing her decision to go ahead with it after all."

The Child grinned from ear to ear. Her small fist shot into the air. "Yes!"

The Crone did likewise. "Yes!" Then, conspiratorially, she finished the explanation. "So then, then she only had to deal with the remaining issue of how to manage creating something she never finished experiencing. That was a toughy. It was a toughy because this second aspect involved the integrity of her work, you understand. She couldn't— wouldn't—present events that never actually happened. Even though the beginning of the sequential meditative experience of our meeting did indeed happen, it never got past that point. You see what I'm saying? So how could she write the finish if it never finished?"

"Yeah, I get it. Mmmm. So?"

"Well! The answer to that dilemma was to do it as a quasi-scientific 'speculative' work."

"A quas . . . . A what?" asked the Child as her face scrunched up like a dried apple.

The Crone laughed. "A quasi-speculative work, Honey. You know, a 'what if' kind of piece that detailed a 'theorized conversation' between us. In the literary field, it was a conceptual work that had never been done before, at least not quite like she ended up presenting it."

"So," the youngster puzzled, "I get all that, but what I'm still wondering is, why'd she change the title? I really liked it when she came up with *Keepers of the Soul*. I loved that title because it was so appropriate, so absolutely, positively excellent! We—you and I—are the keepers of her soul. See, Granny? See what I mean? It was perfect! Why? Why'd she change it?"

Grandma's eyes sparkled as her big smile deepened the crow's feet at the corners. She leaned far over the table toward the Child and whispered, "Because she came up with a title even more appropriate. One far, far more *accurate*."

"Ohhhh," the Child mysteriously whispered back. "What did you say it ended up being?"

"*Trined . . . in . . . Twilight!*"

The Youngster's mind mulled that over. She rolled the strange-sounding title over her tongue like a lemon drop before sliding her eyes up to lock on the elder's. "I don't get it," she whispered.

"What you don't get is how that title fits better than the one you liked. Eh? Maybe you're letting your preference for the former title cloud your thinking. Mmmm? Do you think that could be what's happening, Little Self? Could that be what's keeping you from getting clarity on this?"

"Ummm," the Child hedged, raising her eyes to the ceiling. Then, "Nope, I don't think so. I just plain don't get it."

"Okay then, let me ask you this. Is it that important to get it?

"Yes. I don't like it when I don't understand something. Especially something related to the Mother's works or projects."

"Ahhh, I see. But, Little Self, you know that, sometimes, gaining clarity on certain things—gaining full understanding—doesn't always come on the heels of first learning of that same something. Many times that clarity you seek comes only with the passing of time. All in its own time. Remember?"

This the Child did know. This the Child now accepted with grace, for she knew she would come to an understanding when other elements of the issue all came together—all snuggly fit into their interrelated proper places. So, being a child wise beyond her tender years, she dutifully left the issue without immediately probing further and respectfully accepted the elder's final words on the subject.

Chapter Eleven

The youngster reached for another spiced orange and then cut lengths of both ribbon colors. "I'm going to combine these again," she gaily informed. "I like the way you do yours. I think they look prettiest with both colors together on one pomander."

"Whatever you like," came the reply. "This is your project as well as mine and you can be creative or conforming as you wish."

Wrapping the satin ribbon around the prickly orange, the Child slipped into deep thought once again.

"My, my, Little Self, don't you like my company?" came the unexpected comment from across the table.

That startled the small one out of her reverie. "Oh Granny! How can you even ask that? I love being here with you."

"But your mind is so very far away, Child."

"Only because I've so much to figure out, only because there are so many unanswered questions filling up my mind. The questions, they're filling up all the spaces and spilling out all over the place."

The elder threw her head back in laughter. "Oh Little Self, you're such a joy."

"Joy?" repeated the Child with an exaggerated scowl, "I don't see what's so funny. I don't see what's so hilarious about having a headful of questions, about wanting to know the how's and the why's of things that've happened—that will happen."

"Well, as I distinctly recall, you were planning on setting those things aside while you were here and, later, after you're back in your own time, look at those memories you gained while here." The old one's brow rose. "Mmmm? Didn't you say that you were going to wait to do that?"

The Child didn't reply. The Child was silent.

"Well?" prompted the elder.

Putting the orange down in her lap, the girl rested back in her chair. Giving the one across from her a hard glare, she said, "I can't wait to look at those memories and you already knew that."

"Oh?"

"Yes, you did. You did know that all along. You were just wanting me to come to the same knowing all on my own and now I have."

"You have?"

"Yes. I can't wait until I return to my own time with the Mother to look at all the new memories I now have in this future time because those memories won't be there then. Those memories won't have happened yet—they won't be memories then and I'll have nothing at all to look at."

While the Child made the declaration of her epiphany, the aged fingers nimbly kept up their work, never missing a single beat of the finishing process of the fragrant pomander. She held it aloft, holding it by the ribbon loop and swinging it like a priestess' ceremonial incense burner. "My!" she exclaimed. "Aren't these turning out nice?"

The other nodded. "Yes. Yes, they are. I always loved making these in the fall. But Granny, did you hear what I said?"

"Why, of course, I did, Child, I hear everything. Nothing slips past these old ears. I hear and see everything that goes on in your and the Mother's life . . . feel everything too."

"Well, you didn't comment."

"Was I supposed to? I'm sorry then, were you wanting verification of your own insight, on your own personal revelation? Don't you trust your instincts?"

A heavy sigh came from across the table. The Child slumped in her chair. "Most times I do. I guess I was looking for confirmation but, but," she sputtered, "I suppose I don't need it. Not really. I know I won't remember any of this when I return to the Mother's time."

"Does that upset you? Maybe sadden you somehow?"

"The idea's so new that I think I have to think on it more to even know how I feel about it. All this time I thought I'd go back and remember some of the future and be able to give the Mother some hints and mental nudges in the right direction when she was faced with choices, but, well, now I see that that think'n wasn't right. I won't be able to do that, will I."

"Was that a question, Dear?"

"No, it was a statement of fact, that's all."

Silence.

Waiting.

The clock's pendulum ticked back and forth.

Tick-tock. Tick-tock.

"Granny?"

"Yes?"

"Well?"

"Well, what, Child?"

"I guess I do . . . I guess I do want confirmation."

"Oh," whispered the elder as she reached for another spice-coated orange.

"Oh? That's it? That's all you're going to say?"

"Well, Dear, you're leaving out some related aspects with this, aren't you?"

The youngster's eyes brightened and sparked with renewed hope. "I did?" she asked, while straightening up in her chair and returning to their craft project with renewed vigor.

The old woman nodded. "I believe you did."

"What, Granny? What?"

"Why, the consciousness, Little Self. The answer is in the consciousness and I'm going to give you the wonderful opportunity of thinking this one out for yourself."

The young one's eyes squinted in twinkles along with her sudden wide grin. "Like a game! Like a puzzle in my head!"

"Something like that," came the reply full of amusement over the girl's precociousness.

"Okay," the girl said with bubbling excitement, "you gave me a clue, didn't you?"

"I suppose I did."

"Consciousness," the Child whispered in a voice full of challenge, "the clue's in the consciousness." And her mental gears began spinning and whirring at a furious pace, a pace that kept time with her small hands that worked the orange like an automaton that'd been switched to triple speed production.

Thinking.

Fingers quickly working to wrap the ribbon about the orange and tie the loop off to hang it. Reaching for another orange the small fingers worked in time with the mind.

Thinking.

Working.

Thinking.

Both mind and fingers, working, working.

It was all the wise, old Crone could do to keep from visibly smiling, so heightened was her love for this Child and her bright mind.

"Quantum!" the Child shouted out.

The old one startled. "Oh, my! I told you that you can't scare an old lady like that! Look how you've made me drop my orange!"

Little Self giggled as she stood, palms flat on the table and leaning over it. "That's it! That's it, isn't it? In quantum meditation the Mother—anybody—can go into the future and view stuff—all kinds of stuff!"

"Yes-s-s," came the reply that was prompting further deducements.

"And, and sometimes . . . sometimes left-over effects from those journeys remain behind in the present-day consciousness and show up as things I just know!"

The old one's eyes slowly closed in satisfaction.

"I'm right! I am! That's the answer!" came the youngster's excited squeal. "When I go back my consciousness will retain residuals from our time together! I *will* be able to help Mother out! I'll be able to do that because this time we're sharing together will be a lot like going into quantum meditation!"

The old eyes opened. "But will you need to? Isn't that the real question here?"

Hearing that, the youngster plopped back down in her chair. "What do you mean? I'll know how to help her out with insights, help give her a push in the right direction when decisions need to be made."

Silence.

"Oh, I forgot," sighed the Child, "that's your job."

"Do you think I think you'd be infringing on my job?

"Well . . . wouldn't I be?"

"No, Child, you wouldn't be, you surely wouldn't be. And I wouldn't think you'd be infringing, either. My goodness, you ought to know I'm not that type of person. Between the two of us, any help we can give as guidance to the Mother's purpose is help that benefits the very reason we're here.

"We've always worked together, Dear, and that relationship has always been a smooth-running one—kind of like the perfect partnership. It's not one that makes stepping on each other's toes even a remote possibility. No," came the soft smile, "I certainly don't think you'd be infringing on my job because my job's the same as yours—helping the Mother in whatever way we can. Both of our jobs are to give help whenever either of us perceives a need for it. Whether that help comes from your end or mine isn't even germane. It doesn't make a whit of difference."

The Child liked that answer. Her smile was a happy one that conveyed the acknowledgement of their shared warm camaraderie. "Thanks, Granny," she whispered, "I love you, too."

The old one was so taken aback when she felt her eyes stinging from the impact of the Child's words, she fought back the tears that were beginning to form. Diverting the attention from her welling emotion, she looked over the objects on the table. "Well!" she exclaimed a bit over zealously, "look's like we're all finished here!"

Little Self flung out her arms. "Ta-daaa! We did good on these, didn't we, Granny."

"Oh, yes, Child, we did very good. What say we put all these oranges in a big bowl and clean up our mess."

The girl jumped up and ran to the kitchen cupboard for the paper towels. "I'll do it!"

The old one slowly rose from her chair. "Let's both do it. We seem to work best when we work together."

Chapter Twelve

The two busied themselves, one washing out the spice bowl, the other putting the kitchen table to rights again.

"We did really, really good on those pomanders," declared the Child as she stood back admiring the decorative bowl of fragrant oranges. "I liked the ribbon colors you had for them. They turned out really pretty."

The elder returned from the kitchen and placed her hands on the small shoulders. "I think so too. It was fun, wasn't it?"

"Oh yes, it was lots of fun. Thank you for having a project like that ready for my visit." The youngster turned around and looked up into the other's eyes. "Thank you for thinking of me like that."

"Back atchya! Didn't you also bring a project for us to do? The sage to bundle?"

"Yep!" she squeaked. "I guess we were both thinking the same things. After all," she concluded, "that's only natural for us to do, huh."

"Natural to a point. Natural because we're aspects of the same consciousness, yet both having some uniqueness of individuality. Though we're not separate individuals, we still maintain certain special qualities that are specific to our definitive facets."

The Child understood. "Like you providing the Mother with bits of insightful wisdom and me keeping her childlike qualities strong."

"Yes, exactly. Yet we also have a few individualized inherent traits we can call our own," she said with a special twinkle in her eye, "traits like my patience and your impetuosity."

Though the little one clearly understood that she'd just been lightly chastised, she quickly turned it around. "Balance," she quipped. "We give balance!"

The Crone eyed her.

"Okay, okay," the Child playfully scowled, "I get your meaning. You don't have to say anymore."

"I don't?"

"Nope."

"All right then, what do you think you'd like to do now?"

The Child's eyes scanned the room while she thought about it. "Well, what can we do? I mean, we can't go outside because you said our meeting would end if we did that. So I'm not sure what's allowed."

"Is that what you'd like to do? Go outside?"

The Child nodded. "I like to be outside. When the Mother was little, like me, we spent a lot of time climbing trees and watching nature."

The old woman brought her finger up to her chin and tapped it while deep in thought. "Do you suppose we'd be all right if we stayed inside the garden gate? If we remained in the yard?"

The Child's eyes brightened. "Maybe! Wanna try?"

"Well, it just seems to me that perhaps the garden fence would be our natural perimeter. Wouldn't that seem reasonable to you?"

"Yes, but . . ."

"But?"

"What if it's not? What if we step out there together and then, well, then *poof*," she said, throwing out her arms, "we're *gone*, vanished into thin air?"

"Then we're gone. Then this meeting is over. The question is whether or not both of us want to push the envelope to test it—to take that chance?"

"Ummm," hummed the Child indecisively as she softly drummed her fingertips on the table and thought about the idea. Her eyes, in longing, shifted to the back door. "I want to test it but . . ." she hesitantly added while shyly inching closer to the Crone. Suddenly, clutching the fabric of Granny's long skirt, she added, "then again . . . I don't."

Grandma reached for the Child's hand and led her through the kitchen to stand before the door. "Let's just open this and wait here while we think more on this."

Fresh autumn air wafted inside.

It was inviting.

It was enticing them to step forth.

The two stood side by side and watched the deer mosey back up into the woods.

The old woman spoke first. "The way I see it, you could go out there in the garden area and we'd still be okay."

Little Self seemed to agree. "Yeah, after all, I came up to your door and we were okay. I was outside and you were inside. The biggie question is if you can go outside too?" Her smooth features crinkled in thought. "But shouldn't it be okay? Shouldn't it be okay 'cause you an' me are just alike? We're both aspects of one consciousness?" Then the Child looked up at the Crone and expressed her new bright idea. "How about I just slip outside?" she said, while opening the screen door and cautiously stepping out onto the small porch. "Whaddya think, Granny? Whaddya say I just . . ."

But to her great surprise, the elder was right behind her. "Granny! No! Wait!"

With eyes big as twin full moons, the Child's anxiety turned to wide-eyed wonder. "It worked! Ohhh, it worked! It worked!" And she jumped up and down with uncontained joy as she skipped down the plank steps and danced a jig over the flagstone walkway. Eyes sparkled and laughter rang out as she quickly returned to the steps and grabbed for the old one's outstretched hand. Her voice softened, "C'mon, let's go for a walk!"

The old one met the Child's wild exuberance with a gentle smile. "I slipped out the door like your shadow. Couldn't see the use of prolonging the test. It was either going to work or it wasn't, figured we might as well find out as quickly as possible, eh?"

"But you scared me, Granny," cried the Child. "You really, really scared me! I'd figured we'd take it nice an' slow. You know, like an inch at a time or something. Guess you had other ideas." She grinned. "You fooled me."

"Fooled? Oh, no, not fooled. You had a preconceived notion in your head as to how we'd manage this test. Our notions were just different, is all."

"Well," sighed the little one with relief, "it doesn't matter. I'm just really, really glad it worked all the same." She then pointed to the treeline on the rise beyond the garden gate. "Look, the deer are still here, they're watching us."

"Mmm, they do that now and again. Many times we'll be out here working and, when we look up, they'll be standing up there on that rise watching everything we're doing. Those deer have become like silent neighbors, you know. Though they're silent, they still communicate. They're always around, you just don't always see them."

The two strolled over to the low, lattice garden border fencing and were quiet while they cast their gaze over the fading summer flowers. The new chrysanthemum blossoms brightened the plot with a blaze of brilliant autumn colors.

The Crone sighed. "I do love flowers. Always have. There's something very magical about flower blossoms, don't you think?"

"Uh-huh. I do. The Mother loves flowers, too. She sometimes wishes that she lived in a warmer climate just so she could have flowers blooming all year long. She thinks about that but can never come up with a warmer region that she'd feel comfortable living in. Guess she stays right where she is."

The old one looked down at the Child standing beside her. "Only as long as those probabilities don't change during her life time. While you're here you need to keep that in mind, remember? Everything you see here is based on the choices the Mother is making back in her own time, everything you see is based on the actuality of certain probabilities."

The Child turned her head to look behind her. "Like the river rock on the house," she cleverly cited as an example. "In my time—the Mother's time—the house is made of cedar and now, now it's river rock. I figured the change was due to probabilities or maybe from the effects of the Changes. I also realized that the Boston ivy can only cling to a rock or masonry surface so . . . well, putting a bug in the Mother's ear about it growing successfully right now wouldn't serve any purpose until the river rock was there for it to climb over."

"My, my," commented the elder, "your little mind's been busy, hasn't it?"

The Child shrugged. "Isn't that just logical? The ivy won't stick itself to the cedar wood, so it doesn't begin growing until the river rock's been added." Then Little Self shifted her gaze down the railroad tie steps to the garden below. "That used to be the dog yard."

The old one's brow rose. "Are you going to start harping again on the subject of me getting that new dog?"

"Nope. I didn't say a word. Don't have to because you already promised that you'd think about it."

"And you're just reminding me of that promise."

With firmly set lips, the Child wildly shook her head back and forth. "Nope," she quipped, "not reminding, just stating a fact. That's all I was doing, just stating a fact."

The old woman took the Child's hand. "Let's go down into the lower garden, shall we?"

Descending the steps, the little one voiced an observation about the stairs. "They don't look any older than they do in the Mother's time. Did you replace the ties?"

"Oh, my, no. I just keep staining them with preservative every spring. Replacing them would be far too much work for us now. We're no young chickens anymore, you know. We can still manage to do some of the outside maintenance, but replacing railroad ties is definitely out of the question."

The smaller hand squeezed the larger one. "I think you two do a lot. You do a lot of things most women couldn't do at your . . ."

"My age?"

The Child blushed. "Well, yes. I mean, after all, you're ninety-four and Sally's what, eighty-six now?"

"Mmm, something like that. We don't much care to keep track anymore. Every new year is just another day to us. One day at a time. One blessing at a time. We stopped counting birthdays a long time ago."

The two reached the lower garden area. It was laid out with flagstone walkways separating out the garden plots. Handmade benches were set here and there, and a small gazebo was built into the center. After walking the pathways, they naturally gravitated to the gazebo.

"I like this thing," the Child commented, while sitting on the bench. Peering out the lattice enclosure, she said, "It's sorta cozy, like a cocoon." The windchimes hanging from each side of the structure sent delicate fairy music through the twilight air.

Sitting herself down beside the Child, the Crone also looked about the small shelter. "This was an extravagance for us. We built it ourselves, you know."

"Then why was it an extravagance?"

"Well you ought to know how high the cost of lumber is. My goodness, it took forever for the Mother and Sally to finish off paneling Sally's bedroom. Well," she quipped, "I know that that project hasn't reached your time yet, but it won't be long before it does. One board at a time, you'll see."

"But in my time—in the Mother's time—Sally's mother is still with us."

"Like I said, Child, it won't be long."

The implication of those words were taken to heart. "Oh," was all the little one said, "I get it." Then she was silent for a few minutes before speaking once again. "This lower garden is very pretty, Granny, it feels . . . it feels really peaceful."

"Why do I sense there's a 'but' lurking somewhere in that statement?"

"A but?"

"Mmmm. You heard me."

The Child's shoulders hitched up then fell. "I don't know. Why'd you hear a 'but' in my statement?"

"I heard one because there was one."

"I dunno," came the little white lie.

"I do. You think this lower garden is very beautiful, yet think it was much better the way it was before—as a dog yard."

"Maybe."

"I said I'd think about it. Isn't that enough? What, you want me to sign it in blood?"

Hearing that, the Child laughed. "Granny, that was so silly."

"Well, I certainly thought so too!"

The chimes softly tinkled like fragile fairy bells.

The forest was alive with the birds' sweet evensong.

"All the birds are saying their goodnights," whispered Little Self in a voice heavy with deepest respect.

"That they are, Child. To me it's one of the most beautiful sounds in the world. There's such a magical feel to being outside in twilight and listening to the crisp sounds of a day's end ringing out from one end of the forest to the other. It's such an incredibly peaceful sound, isn't it? It's like a prayer—nature chanting its evening vespers. Oh, yes, this has always been a very sacred time of day for me, a time when nature prayed."

"Could that be why twilight is such a magical time," inquired the Child.

"Well, I never thought about it but, now that you mention it, I surely wouldn't doubt it. Although the word you want is sacred instead of magic. Sometimes the two get mixed up."

The little one smiled. "That's what I think. I think nature's prayers can give a magical feel to nature's sacredness."

"That's a good thought. I like that idea. Maybe so, Little Self, maybe so."

And the two fell into a silent reverie while listening to nature's sweet and lilting evensong.

The youngster was greatly enjoying the tranquillity of the moment—of the place—yet she had so much on her mind that the many thoughts crowding her mind were creating a distraction.

The old woman, wanting very much to share the garden's deep serenity with the child, sensed that the serenity was being shattered by the young one's spinning mental gears.

"Dear One," she whispered, placing a hand on the patched fabric of the small knee and tenderly massaging the little joint beneath, "must you always let your mind race so?"

The Child blew out an exaggerated breath. "It's not that I do it on purpose," she grimaced. "It just happens all by itself! Maybe I got it from the Mother when she was little. She was always thinking, thinking, thinking of all sorts of things like possibilities, like the What Ifs to life, like the elements and philosophies that society saw as being puzzles and mysteries. When she was my age she was questioning so many things about life, because those things didn't seem so puzzling to her. She even puzzled why people puzzled over them!

"I guess I just got this curiosity from her when she'd climb up into that big apple tree in the backyard and sit for hours on end thinking about the mysterious aspects of life that really never seemed so mysterious to her. She's the one who got me into the habit. It's all her fault. I got the habit from her. Do you think it's a bad habit? Is that what you're getting at?"

"Oh, absolutely not! Thinking is a wonderful tool to discovery! But Dear, here we are down in this peaceful garden and instead of enjoying it to the fullest, your mind is spinning like a falling star. May I ask what's on your mind?"

Sheepishly, the little one's cheeks flushed. "You'll think I'm being silly if I tell you."

"And why would you think that?"

"Because it's so off the wall, that's why."

"Some of the best questions are those folks think are off the wall. Why don't you give me a try. Mmmm? Surely it can't be all that silly."

The Child scrunched up her mouth while debating what to do. "It really is off the wall."

"So?"

"Okay, then. But only if you promise you won't laugh when I tell you."

"I can't make promises, but I'll try to keep a straight face," teased the Crone. "Okay now, out with it. Shoot."

"Well? Actually I was thinking about clones."

"Clones," the old woman softly echoed. "Oh-kaayy. Clones as in the flower variety of clones or clones as in the human variety of clones?"

The small fingers nervously twisted a piece of loose thread hanging off her bib overall button. "As in the human variety."

"And?"

Silence.

Waiting.

The Child's eyes diverted from the Crone's to scan the garden. "I like that angel statue over there. She's holding a seashell full of birdseed. So do the birds actually come and eat from it?"

"All the time," replied the elder, recognizing that the Child was temporarily detouring around the former subject matter. "All the time," she repeated. "Half my days are taken up with filling all the feeders we have about the place. Between the deer bowls over by the birdbath, the raccoon bowls and sunflower troughs on the front porch, the hanging feeders, and these in the garden, I've my hands full just keeping up with the hungry critters. Never want to let them go empty for any amount of time or you'll disappoint them." The Crone winked. "They've come to depend on all of their routine dinner plates being full, you know."

"I know," the Child smiled. "Back in my time Sally

sometimes calls our place 'Rain's Diner.' You know, a regular place to eat for the critters. Does she still say that?"

"Ohh, once in awhile I still hear that comment."

"Thought so."

"And did you also think you'd changed the subject so smoothly that an old woman hadn't noticed?"

The Child's head bowed. "Oh, that. You did notice."

"Of course, I noticed. Did you think I was senile?"

"Well . . . maybe." Then she giggled, "Nooo, I was just kidding."

"Well!" the Crone huffed with playful exaggeration. "I most certainly hope so!"

"Anyway, Granny, that wasn't fair to ask if I thought you were senile. Why . . . your mind's as sharp as a pine needle!"

"Humph," the old woman muttered, "it has to be with you running around in it."

That brought a huge playful grin from the Child. "And you love it, too! You love it because I'm the one keeping *you* young, isn't that right, Granny."

"Oh, yes, indeed," came the reply as Grandma scanned the sky. "You surely are the one keeping me on my toes, never letting my consciousness forget the more fun-loving aspects of life." Then her eyes made a sweep of the garden until they moved far enough around to meet up with the youngster's. "I believe," she cooed, "we were talking about clones—people clones."

"Oh, all right," Little Self conceded, "told you your mind was sharp as a pine needle."

"Just don't you forget it," teased the Crone.

"How can I? You won't let me." Sighing, Little Self said, "I had a question about it and I was scared to keep asking and asking things of you. I kinda felt like I was bugging you for answers to things all the time."

"Few learn without asking questions, Dear. Besides, the

Grand Canyon lies between 'bugging' someone and just having a plain old friendly discussion on a wide variety of 'conversational topics.'"

"Well, yes, I know that, but I don't want you to think that I think you're some kind of walking encyclopedia or something. Know what I mean?"

"I do." Then Grandma leaned down and gave the Child a conspiratorial sideglance. "Most encyclopedias won't have the answers to the type of special questions you have. Those books won't even have thought of the primary questions! How can answers be given if the questions themselves haven't even come to mind? No, Dear," the Crone assured, patting the girl's knee, "I surely don't think you think I'm some walking encyclopedia. Why don't you give it a shot and we'll see what kind of answer we can come up with, see if it's suitable or not."

The young one rolled her eyes, chest heaving and falling with her big sigh. "Okay, here goes nothin'."

"You go for it then we'll see if it's nothin' or not."

Taking a big breath, Little Self went for it. "When I hear the Mother sometimes wish she had a clone of herself because she always has so much to do and not enough time to do it in, it got me wondering about the subject. So . . . I was wondering, well, if a human was cloned it wouldn't really be a true clone. I decided that it'd be an impossibility, human cloning, I mean."

"It would? It'd be an impossibility?"

"Sure it would."

"And what makes you deduce that?"

"Spirits. Every human has a separate spirit—even a clone, once it reached its biological fetal maturity and the umbilical was cut. Do you see what I mean?"

Grandma did. She let the Child finish her premise by prompting her to continue. "Yes, I see. Go on."

"Well, the way I see it, the DNA of the original human being would be exactly the same as her or his new clone, but the *spirit* of the new human—the clone—would carry the imprinted aspects of all its *own* past lives. It would be different. Its personality traits, inclinations, astrological signs it was born under, etc., would all be different and affect the clone in a wide variety of ways that would make it lots different than the human host. That's why nobody could be an exact replica of another. That's why nobody could have a perfect clone of herself."

Silence.

Waiting.

Deeper silence.

"Well, Granny? Whaddya think?"

"I think, Little Self," the old woman lovingly exclaimed, "that you continue to amaze me. That was extremely astute thinking. Of course you're right on the money with this, you know. So, Smarty, what's the bottom line philosophy here? What's it all mean?"

The Child's eyes literally glimmered with dancing twilight reflections. She felt that glowing fullness of heart that comes from knowing someone you love is proud that you'd done a good job at something. "The bottom line is that one's *consciousness* cannot be cloned! There are no two identical consciousnesses that exist or . . . ever will. That's the impossibility. That's the impossibility of trying to clone a human."

The elder slowly closed her eyes and nodded. "Exactly." Opening them, she searched the Child's shining eyes. "Even identical twins can share like DNA but never . . . never like consciousnesses. The biological elements can be cloned, but never the mind itself, for that alone is what makes each and every one of us unique and diversely separate from one another. A human clone will never think the same as its original host. Though it'll look exactly the same, it'll never be the same."

"That's because it has a different, separate spirit, huh Granny," underscored the little one.

"Yes, that's because it has a different, separate spirit that carries its own unique, vast array of diverse past-life experiences that greatly differentiate it from its own biological host."

The Child was pensive as she thought about the concept and the wonderful verification that came after expressing her theory.

The Grandma looked down at her. "May I ask why or how this subject came to mind?"

"Sure. Remember when I said that I'd sometimes heard the Mother express a wish for a clone of herself so she could get more done in less time?"

"Mmmm. I remember."

"Well, that's what got me thinking about the whole thing. Even if the Mother could clone herself, the clone wouldn't really be a duplicate of her. Physically, it'd look just like her but it'd have a mind of its own." Little Self then locked an intent gaze upon the elder's wise eyes and made a distasteful face. "That'd never do. That'd just never do. That'd be awful, wouldn't it?"

"Oh, most awful, indeed!"

"Anyway, this dumb cloning stuff got me thinking. It got me thinking about how folks aren't thinking about it, at least when it comes to cloning human beings. They're missing the main part of the issue. They're forgetting all about the consciousness. They're still way behind when they don't—or won't—separate the touchable brain from the untouchable consciousness. So, right there, right there is where they get onto the wrong track. Right there is when they goof up and think that a cloned brain will contain the host's same consciousness when . . . when it never will or ever could have."

"This is true, Child. And it goes to prove the importance of technology—advances and discoveries—keeping in step with wisdom, with expansive logic, and with solid reasoning. They must be tandem components to scientific discovery. One without the others creates chaos. One without the others takes society backwards instead of moving forward toward its goal of intellectual advancement."

The Child put her feet up on the edge of the redwood bench and hugged her legs. Chin resting on the knobby knees, she didn't hesitate to ask the next most logical question, "Have they gone and done it? In the time between my time and yours, have they done it anyway?" Then, without waiting for the answer, she harumphed, "They have, haven't they?"

"They have. They managed to do it and, at the same time, had managed to create a head-scratching dilemma as to why the clones and hosts were not exactly the same. And the experiments increase in their effort to find the solution that plagues their days by continually eluding them."

"That's not logical to me."

"Why's that?"

"Because back in the Mother's time scientists had just determined—discovered—that all of life is connected by a cosmic or universal type of consciousness . . . The Great Web of Life. If they'd gotten that far back then, why wouldn't it be a natural conclusion for them to come to with the minds of clones?" The Child shook her head in puzzlement. "That doesn't make any sense because that conclusion should've naturally followed when related to the issue of human clones."

"Ahhh," sighed the old woman, "those should'ves, would'ves, could'ves don't always come into the big picture when dealing with new concepts and experimental research done in other areas of endeavor. Those theories that have been proven and withstood the test of time are often left outside the perimeters of new research. In essence, they've forgotten those discovered elements or else they've not realized that they need to be factored in."

"That's just plain stupid, Granny. That's just so ignorant. Stupid, stupid, stupid!"

"Well," Grandma muttered sullenly, "maybe so, Child. Maybe so."

"Maybe so?" came the somewhat indignant reply.

"Yes, maybe so. Don't forget, Dear, researchers are human. I'm not saying that that's an excuse, but it is a reason sometimes. Forgetting dynamic elements to a new realm of discovery or experiment is not a rarity. Eventually they'll figure it out and get it right. Eventually their present-day mystery will be solved."

"But what about in the meantime? In the meantime the scientific community is creating physically identical twins of people. I worry that they might also think these twins—the clones—don't have a soul! They don't treat them like auto . . . auto . . . robots, do they?"

The Crone smiled. "Automatons. No, not now, they don't."

Little Self was incredulous. "You mean they actually did?"

"At first the scientists didn't quite know what to make of their first success. They argued over whether this newly-created twin of the host was a real human being or some type of prototype. The scientific ethicists debated for quite some time over the issue. Oh," she chuckled, "those debates were hot ones! Whew! They went on and on. Then, it was finally determined that a human clone was indeed a real human being based on the fact that it was biologically created just as a human fetus was.

"But then," she exclaimed with a raised brow, "then the issue of the soul came into the equation and a new enigma was created for them. Science was forced to address spirituality and . . ."

"And they still didn't get it. They still didn't reconcile the two, did they?"

"No. No, they didn't. They still don't get the fact that one's consciousness is the individual spirit of that person, that a person's spirit and consciousness are one and the same."

"So?" Little Self eagerly asked, looking up at Grandma. "So what'd they do? What'd they come up with to justify the differences between the host and clone?"

"I think you didn't need to ask that question. I think you already know."

"The mind. They're still hung up on the mind being the touchable brain. They concluded that the mind is what makes the host and clone different. They still don't get the difference between the physical brain and nonphysical consciousness—the spirit."

"See? I told you that you didn't have to ask me that question."

A heavy sigh escaped from the Child's lips. "Jeez," was all she could think to say.

The Crone didn't hesitate to second the response with her own quiet sigh. "Jeez is right." Then she patted the small knees. "As I said before, some changes since the Mother's time have been good ones—really good ones, and," she paused, "some have not been so great. Then again, after all these years, some things haven't changed at all." Casting her gaze along the treeline, she said, "No, ma'am, some things haven't changed at all. Not one, single, tiny whit."

Little Self tenderly covered the Crone's hands with her own. "Does that make you sad, Granny?"

"Sad? Oh, sometimes, I suppose it does. But as with all things, we have to have acceptance of how things are. Realizations can't be forced. Discovery and intellectual growth often comes slowly. So until science and spirituality stop flirting with one another, end their long engagement, and get down to the serious business of committing to their marriage, acceptance of their procrastination is the only way to endure the situation."

A small hand sympathetically patted the gnarled one.

There was nothing more to be said.

Chapter Thirteen

A semicircle of mountain ridges curved around the two sitting in the garden gazebo like Mother Nature's gentle hands protectively cradling two newborn fawns and, from their depths, a call rang out.

Little Self smiled up at the one sitting beside her and whispered, "A nighthawk."

The elder had her eyes closed as if in deep meditation. She slowly opened them. "Yes," she whispered back. "The woods are in transition now. The night ones are just beginning their day. If you look to your left, up in the top of that pine, you'll see another who's been watching us for some time now."

The Child grinned and turned her head to spy the surprise. "Why, hello, Mrs. Owl," she joyfully greeted. "How're you this fine evening? Are you terribly confused by this extended twilight time?"

"Hoot! Hoo-hoo-oot!"

Laughing, the young one was about to pose a like question to her companion. "Granny?"

"I don't know," came the reply.

The Child perked up. Her legs unfolded and dangled off the bench. Hands smartly snapping to her hips, she quipped, "Wait a minute. I haven't asked my question yet." Then she narrowed her eyes in suspicion. "Is all this like some kind of instant replay for you?"

The old one's hands mimicked the youngster's. With an equally over-dramatized aghast expression, she replied, "Is that what you think?"

"Oops, guess not," Little Self sheepishly responded, "but you answered my question before I even asked it. What was I to think?"

"You couldn've started by thinking your question was a most logical one following in the footsteps of what you'd asked that owl up there. Huh?" she asked while raising her brow higher and higher. "Mmmm? It appeared to me that you'd asked that old owl something that you'd also want to ask an old woman?"

"And you just knew that, didn't you."

"Indeed. That's all it was, Little Self, that's all it was. Nothing more esoteric and nothing less than naturally antic- ipating your next question. Tsk-tsk," she softly clucked, "you've got to watch your assumptions closer than that."

The Child hung her head.

The old woman reached down to raise the small chin. "Now none of that either. None of that self-pity nonsense. So you jumped to a conclusion that was based on a false assumption? So? Leave it be and learn from it. After all, Dear, you can't take the words back so make them useful— turn them into a lesson learned, one used as a reminder for the next time. My goodness," she sighed, "it's not like we can't all use those little prompter lessons now and again, eh?"

The little one smiled. "Uh-huh." Then her legs began to swing back and forth again. "So! You really don't know the answer to my question?"

"Tell you what, why don't we start this all over again. Go ahead," she urged, "ask your question."

"This is silly," grinned the Child.

"So who says we can't be silly? Go ahead. Ask."

"But now I feel stupid about it because you already know what I'm going to ask."

"Questions are never stupid. So pretend I don't know what you're going to ask. What, you don't know how to pretend anymore? Where's your imagination gone to? You used to have a wonderfully creative imagination, you know. Why, I can remember when you . . ."

"Okay! Okay! I'll ask it!" While feeling a bit self-conscious (and silly), she straightened herself up and pasted on the serious face of a mime. She cleared her throat and announced. "Actually, I have two questions."

"Two," the other echoed.

"Yes, two. The first one is the same one I asked the owl. Is nature confused by this prolonged state of twilight we've caused?"

"Oh."

"Oh?"

"Well. I suppose I jumped the gun then, didn't I? Earlier I'd answered your second question."

The Child loved that. One corner of her mouth tipped up before covering the full-blown smile with her hand. She mumbled through the fingers, "Would that have been an example of someone making an assumption?"

"Well," the old one spouted beneath a returned grin, "I suppose you could call it one of those 'reminders' we were talking about. Yes," she admitted, "I guess it was an assumption. Touché, Child. You got me!"

Embarrassed, the little one hid her face in the elder's faded skirt fabric. When she raised her head, the cheeks were blushing. "Nobody's perfect, Granny."

"Oh, my, Dear Heart, don't I know it! You get to be ninety-four that's one thing in life you're absolutely certain of!" She rested her hand upon the small one. "That's one golden truism, all right. I may be the Mother's Higher Self, but that doesn't mean I never get ahead of things once in a while." She winked, "That's something I've got to watch."

Little Self giggled. "We both have things to watch, don't we, Granny."

"Oh, yes, indeed we do, Child, indeed we do. So! Shall we get on with your questions?"

Little Self nodded and repeated her question. "Is nature confused by this extended twilight time?"

"No. No, I think not because it's really not a true extension. Time is still ticking along while we're together, the footsteps of time are still marching on their merry way. The clock's hands have not stopped moving at the twilight hour. The pendulum still swings. The hour still chimes."

"Suspended?" the Child interjected her alternate word for the concept. "Time has just been suspended?"

"Ahhh, now that's good, yes. Suspended."

"So nature isn't really experiencing the passing of time, it's just existing within a frozen moment of it." The Child's head tilted in doubt. "That didn't sound quite right."

"Probably because you used the word 'frozen.' That sounds awfully stodgy—cold. Time isn't really frozen, it's only . . . well, paused would be a more appropriate term. It's paused, you see."

"Paused! Yes, that's the word I was looking for. So . . . " she pondered, " . . . nature can't be confused when it doesn't even know that the twilight is being paused. Nature doesn't know that time stopped ticking, umm, paused in twilight for a little while. Nature—all the critters—are just living in an extended twilight time that they don't even realize is being prolonged. Is that it? Is that right?"

"You got it. Now, about that second question that I can't answer. You may as well go ahead and ask that one as well."

Without hesitation, the Child voiced it. "How far does this paused twilight extend? I mean . . ."

"Oh, I know what you mean. I know exactly what you're wondering. You want to know if this paused twilight time is just around this property or if it extends out into the world. Mmm? Is that it?"

Little Self nodded.

"And I'm sorry to say that I can't answer that with any absolute knowledge because this is the first time this kind of meeting has been accomplished. This is all brand new." The Crone smiled down at the youngster. "We've set a precedent in the spiritual realm, Child. You know that, don't you?"

"I haven't really thought about it, but I guess we have."

"Well, anyway, logically speaking, it wouldn't be at all reasonable to think that we've paused time everywhere. I tend to think there's some type of boundary or certain perimeter where this twilight is encapsulated within. What do you think?"

"I think so too. Maybe just your property."

"Maybe so."

The two thought about it for several quiet moments before the little one spoke. "Do you think the abbey is included in this?"

"It's not that far away. I would think the abbey would be included, yes."

"Then, then would anyone who's visiting it realize what was happening?"

"No."

"That was fast. How can you be so sure?"

"I don't know how I know, I just do. Some things are like that, you know."

The Child's eyes crinkled with her smile. "Yes, I know. The Knowing."

Chapter Fourteen

Somewhere from within the gray depths of the forest the nighthawk called out again. Across the valley its mate returned the cry.

"This is my absolute, bestest, favorite time of day," commented the little one.

"Mmm, mine too. I always thought there was a special kind of mystical sensation associated with it. At least that's what I've always felt about it. How about you?"

"Oh, yes! Well . . . I guess we know that to be true now, don't we, Granny."

"I suppose we do."

The two rested well within each other's presence. Silences, even long ones, were not an uncomfortable feeling. Some of the silences spoke more than the words did because they were golden ones shared by two of one mind.

"Stones," Little Self whispered.

"Eh? What was that?"

"Oh, I was just looking up at the house. It seems so strange not seeing the cedar siding."

"Don't forget, this place is a place of probabilities, Dear. That's what its made of. Every decision the Mother and Sally make in their time—your time—affects what this place looks like. The river rock stones came about when some reinforcing was required due to the structural damage from the geologic events."

"I figured that out when you'd said that you had to make some repairs to the place. I just never expected to see it so changed. Well, not really so changed, just different. I mean, it's basically still the same place."

"Yes, it is. But remember the fact that different probabilities manifesting in the Mother's time could make additional changes to this place. For instance, if the geologic events were more severe in this area, perhaps the place wouldn't be standing at all. Or if they were less severe perhaps the exterior would still be cedar right now. Keep these things in mind while you're here."

"I guess I automatically do. I understand about probabilities. Especially since this is the future. I really do understand, Granny."

"Good, I'm glad to hear that."

"Anyway," the Child said, returning to her original thought. "I was thinking of stones, especially of the river rock. The Mother used to live in a tiny stone cabin and she really loved that place."

"Yes, I remember it. As I recall, she'd bought it to use just as a writing cabin. That's why it was so small. She'd never intended to actually live in it, so it didn't need to be much larger than a shoebox."

"That's funny. A shoebox."

"Well, it was small, wasn't it?"

"Yeah, it was small, all right. That's the place where I first talked to Sally. That's after the Mother had to move into it and live there."

"Is this conversation going somewhere specific because, if it's not, don't you think we have happier pastimes to reminisce about?"

"Uh-huh. I didn't intentionally go there. I was meaning to talk about how much she loves stone houses. Small stone cottages and living offshore. That's where I was going. Remember when she lived right off the shore of Lake Superior?"

"Oh, indeed I do! She was there for six months, if I recall."

"Five. From October to March."

The old one thought on that. "You're right, it was just five months, but she did love that little place. Are you wondering if she ever got the chance to live by the water again?"

"Well . . . I was. But I suppose if she's still in this place in 2040, then she never lived anywhere else. Would that be a correct conclusion? I mean, that wouldn't just be an assumption based on circumstantial evidence, would it?"

"Actually, it could be both."

"Both?"

"Sure. If this is still her dwelling in 2040 you could be assuming that she never lived anywhere else based on that alone. Yet, what if she closed up this place for a time and, for a change of scene, went to live elsewhere? You didn't factor in that probability. Just because she lives in this spot in her time and we're still in it in 2040 doesn't mean she couldn't have lived somewhere else in between. Mmm?"

The Child nodded. "I didn't take enough time to think it through. So did she?"

"Did she what?"

Little Self sighed and flashed the old one an exasperated look. "You know. Did she live somewhere else in between? Did she ever get to live by the shore again?"

"She does love the water."

"Granny!"

"Yes, Dear, she did."

Relief was visible by the Child's widening grin. "Oh, I'm so glad. I almost wish she could've stayed there . . . wherever 'there' was. I remember how much she came to love hearing the sound of the fog horns and the buoy bells clanging in the night. And how the waves in winter made magical ice caves offshore, how she'd climb on them and peer down into the water churning beneath their caverns, how she walked for hours on end along that sandy beach. We had lots of fun there. I liked it too. Did she live by one of the big lakes or an ocean?"

"Oh, Little Self, tsk-tsk, no ocean."

"I didn't think so."

The Child's body language told of her building excitement.

Seeing it, the Crone cautioned, "Now remember what I told you . . . about those probabilities. Don't you go getting yourself all worked up about something that may change when the time for a certain decision comes about."

Little Self stilled her fidgeting hands. "I know. I know. What else? What else, Granny?"

"What do you mean, what else? You want me to tell you everything that happened in forty years?"

"Well, no. That'd really be silly because they may not happen that way at all. I just got really excited to know that maybe—maybe—we'll live by the water again, at least for a little while."

"Just keep that 'maybe' in mind, that's all."

"Okay."

The Crone suspiciously eyed the girl. "You're not giving me lip service, are you?"

"I wouldn't do that, Granny. I'll remember that all of this," she said, flinging her arm about the garden, "all of this is one big, gigantic Maybe. So, what's the Great Nothing all about?"

"My goodness, Child, don't you even take a breath between questions? Between subject matters?"

The question was greeted by a wide grin. "Since neither of us knows how long this twilight time is going to stay paused for us, I thought I'd better get in as many questions as I can. So, what's the deal with the Mother's Great Nothing feeling she gets? What's it mean? Where does it come from?"

The old one released a long, extended sigh. "Ahh, you don't like that, do you. You don't like it when she gets that dark feeling."

"No! I hate it! It's so . . . so ickky!"

Hearing that description, the elder's eyes lit up with laughter.

The Child was offended. She jumped up and began prancing before the old one. "What's so funny? Did I say something funny? It is ickky. It's dark and . . . and it's spooky! It's scary, that's what it is. And it's not only me who hates it, she does too!"

The young one's wild animations and honest sincerity endeared the old one to the Child even more than she'd thought possible.

"Come here, Honey," she softly said, patting her skirt. "Come sit on my lap. Let me hold you."

"No! I don't want to be held. I want to know what causes the Great Nothing!"

"I heard you the first time. Perhaps if you'd stop pacing back and forth like a woman waiting for her first grandchild to be born we could talk about it." Again she patted her lap. "Mmm? Would that be a good idea?"

The Child halted in midstep to consider the idea. "Would it be all right if I went back inside and got my dolly?"

"I don't see why not. I'll just wait here for you."

Turning and racing up the steps two at a time and letting the screen door slam behind her, the young one was back in a flash with Raggedy Ann. Panting, she stood before grandma. "We can sit on your lap now."

The old Crone smiled while the Child comfortably situated herself sideways to distribute her weight across the other's lap.

The elder waited.

And waited.

"Are you quite done fidgeting?" she finally asked.

"Yes," Little Self informed in a dignified manner. "Quite done."

"Good. I'm so glad to hear that. Now, about this Great Nothing that you say feels so ickky and spooky . . ."

The Child had calmed down. She sighed, " . . . It's ickky and spooky because it comes with the feeling that there's no tomorrow." Fingering the doll's apron and smoothing out its wrinkles, she quietly admitted, "I don't like it when there's that no-tomorrow feeling. That's what's so scary about it."

"Yes, that certainly would be a scary feeling, all right."

"So I thought that if I understood what the Great Nothing was caused by, I wouldn't be so upset by it when it comes over the Mother."

"That's logical reasoning. Most fears vanish once they're thoroughly understood. Little Self," Grandma whispered, while brushing off a speck of dirt from the doll's face, "even the Mother doesn't know the reason for her Great Nothing feeling."

"I know," the Child whispered back, "but you do, don't you."

Wisps of silver strands wafted about her head like fairy dust when the old woman nodded. "Oh, yes, indeed, that I do."

A small finger touched a button on the elder's blouse. "You have a broken button," she informed her.

Grandma's hand rose to her chest and gently wrapped around the Child's. "I have many broken buttons, but they still work. They may not look so great but nobody sees me anymore and it really doesn't matter." Then her voice softened. "Child?"

"What?"

Grandma peered into the rich, mahogany eyes that appeared to be avoiding contact. "Now that you have the opportunity to find out what causes this Great Nothing, are you feeling a little reluctant to make that discovery? Are you scared to find out the reason for it?"

"A little. A little because I don't want you to tell me that the Mother gets this feeling because she's sensing her death or something horrible like that. I'm afraid you're going to say that that's the reason."

"Ohhh, dear, Dear Heart!" the old woman cooed, while wrapping her thin arms firmly about the Child and giving her a long, warming hug. She stroked the little one's parted hair. "Dear God, no wonder you were jumping all about with this question. No wonder you were so concerned. My goodness, it's nothing like that. It's nothing like that at all!"

Little Self raised her head.

Tears were about to spill over.

Grandma wiped them away with her skirt. "There, there."

With relief at Granny's revelation and seeing her use her skirt in such a way, the Child sniffed and gave a nervous giggle. "The Mother wipes tears away with her skirt, too."

Grandma grinned. "I know. We've been doing it for years. These old calico skirts have more uses than you can shake a stick at. There," she said after wiping the other eye, "all dry."

"Thank you."

"You're quite welcome. Now. Let's get to the point here. This Great Nothing feeling the Mother sometimes gets doesn't come from her sensing that she's going to die. Just because the feeling carries the sense of there being no tomorrow doesn't mean death. Understand?"

The Child nodded.

"Okay, I want to be sure you do understand that."

"I do," the little one sniffled.

In an attempt to lighten the somber mood, the Crone again raised up the bottom of her skirt. "Need to blow your nose?"

Little Self erupted in wild laughter. "Oh Granny! Yuck! That's awful! Ohh, yuck! The Mother never uses her skirt for that!"

Lowering the skirt grandma admitted, "Well, I'll share a wee secret with you, neither do I. And I agree, that'd really be yucky, wouldn't it. I just thought we could use a spot of humor about now. Life's just no fun without a good daily dose of humor."

"Granny?"

"Mmm?"

"I really like you."

"I really like you, too, Little Self," she said tenderly. "I really do. You are a sweet, precious, precious child."

The youngster's cheeks blushed and so she quickly changed the subject. "So! If impending death—or a strong probability of it—isn't the reason for the Mother's Great Nothing feeling, what is?"

Silence.

Waiting.

"Granny?"

"I'm coming, I'm coming," she said after mentally putting her thoughts in order. "After giving it further consideration,

I'd have to say a *type* of death *is* the cause for the Great Nothing feeling she gets."

"Oh, no," Little Self whispered.

"Now don't go jumping into those assumptions again. What I'm talking about is a sense of futility that comes over her at times—the death of her words, Little Self, of her *words*."

Little Self's mouth downturned with a frown. "I don't get it."

"Wait a minute, I'm not done explaining. You see, when she sees evidence of people twisting her words all out of shape and making wild assumptions, she naturally feels that the words—the messages—were futile to give. It's a sense of the purity of the words being sullied or compromised by people's gross misinterpretations and, therefore, being likened to the true meaning of those words being killed—not living their integrity throughout all the tomorrows. See what I'm saying?"

Sadly, the Child responded with deep empathy. "Yes, I see," she muttered. "I see now how that would fit, how that would give her the feeling of a Great Nothing in respect to her life's work. It'd make her feel like she wasn't effective or that, somehow, she was doing something wrong since she had a feeling that her words were dying."

Grandma fingered the curled up end of one of the long braids. "I'm sorry you thought the reason for this might be the Mother sensing her own death. That must've been very upsetting for you."

"I should've been more perceptive. I should've realized it was connected to her work because I know the Mother doesn't fear her own death." Then the small mouth pursed into a pout and spouted, "Sometimes I just hate people!"

"Oh nooo, Little Self, don't say that. Please, don't say that, Honey. You don't really hate people, you only hate how they behave. It's their behavior that you sometimes hate."

"Same thing," the Child defended.

"Oh, no. No, no. No, it's not!"

"Well some people have been so mean to her! They make up all kinds of nasty lies and then say that those lies came from her! I hate them, Granny, I just hate them!"

"Shhh. Shhhh," the old one soothed with a calming hug.

Tears began brimming again as the Child vented her sense of rightness. "But it's not right! What right do people have to be so mean to someone who never did or said a mean thing in her life? It's so unfair!"

While the elder again reached for the bottom of her skirt, she softly said, "Sticks an' stones, Little Self. Sticks and stones."

"Sticks and stones! Sticks and stones hurt!"

"No, not the verbal kind. Those only hurt if they're internalized by the victim herself," she reminded while wiping the wetness from the Child's cheeks. "Verbal stoning doesn't have to leave a single mark, not when it's ignored and seen for what it truly is.

"Honey," she soothed, "all the verbal meanness in the world, all that twisting of the Mother's words that people do, and all the false accusations and gossip can run off her like water off a mallard's pretty back."

"But it doesn't always do that! It hurts! Otherwise the Great Nothing wouldn't come over her like it does."

"Hold on there. Just a minute. I believe you're transferring here. You're transferring your *own* feelings to her because it does run off her back, Little Self, it does. But I don't think it runs off yours. Mmm?

"You see, Honey, it's not her she's concerned about, it's the words. It's when the words and concepts get twisted and misshapened that makes her feel that people are killing the message—its purity. There's a big difference here. And it's that difference that makes her feel that her message has fallen into a Great Nothing space. It's that difference that sometimes gives her a sense of futility of purpose—a death of purpose. It's got nothing to do with herself, per se. Do you understand?"

"I understand how you've explained the Great Nothing but I don't understand why people have a need to be mean and feel they need to search for faults in others. And if they can't find any faults they make them up. It's those kinds of things I don't understand, Granny. Why can't people be nice? Why can't they just be nice to each other? Why can't they see that it's so much more fun being nice than mean? Why can't they see that practicing unconditional goodness is so much better and uplifting than choosing to behave with unconditional hatred? Where have all the pure hearts gone, Granny? Where?"

Silence.

"Granny? Where?"

"Ohh, honey, they're still around. Believe me, they're still around and always will be, have no fear of that."

"Well," the Child huffed, "I sure don't see a great preponderance of them."

The old Crone suddenly raised a cautioning brow. "Now don't you go getting cynical on me with your big hundred-dollar words."

"Preponderance is not a big word. I hear the mother use it all the time. Besides, it fits. It's a perfect word," she strongly declared. "And another thing that I just thought of, I bet the Mother doesn't finish the *Starborn* trilogy novels because of how people twist things." She held up Raggedy Ann. "And I bet you my doll that she also doesn't do the *Song of Sophia* book either because some stupid people started spreading the false rumor that she was claiming to be some goddess! I'm right, aren't I, Granny. I know I am. There would be no way she'd do that book after she heard those lies starting."

The old one exhaled a deep, extended sigh. "Yes, Little Self, you're right."

"I knew it. I just knew it!"

"The *Sophia* book was the only one she refused to publish due to people's twisted reactions to her previous works. Remember, Little Self, she did put those three other manuscripts back on her computer and ended up publishing them. But then, after she saw how folks made up stories about her and the things she supposedly claimed or implied, there was no way she was going to add fuel to the lies by doing the personal interpretation of the *Thunder, Perfect Mind* gnostic gospel." The elder's eyes misted. "It would've been so beautiful, Little Self. It would've been so beautifully moving and revealing."

"See? See! That's why I hate people!"

"Please, Little Self, please don't do that."

The small shoulders slumped. "Well . . . okay then, that's why I hate people's mean behavior."

The old woman warmly wrapped her arms about the distraught Child. She held her firmly and hugged tight. Together they rocked back and forth. "Little Self, the Mother has worked hard to dispel hatred and intolerance from the world. Please, please promise me you'll never hate anyone, that you'll *never* hate anyone."

No response.

"Honey?" Grandma prompted with a whisper.

Silence.

Then the old woman gave a gentle reminder. "Isn't that the least we can do to help manifest the Mother's message? To honor all her hard work? To take to heart all her messages about stopping the intolerance and hatred?"

Thinking.

Waiting.

"Hating," Little Self mumbled with honesty. "It's a hard thing not to do sometimes."

"Nobody said it was easy," Grandma gently reminded. "Anything worth doing is worth putting all one's effort into."

Silence.

The nighthawk called.

And when the answer finally came, it came as a softly hushed, baby's breath whisper—a whisper filled with the integrity of an innocent child's pure heart. "I promise, Granny. I promise."

Chapter Fifteen

A wise old woman and a precocious little girl sat together in the solemn twilight while the deep woods of the surrounding mountainsides rustled with the stirrings of nature awaiting the coming nightfall.

The girl turned her head to watch the owl silently glide from its perched position in the lodgepole pine, then she gave her attention to the old one sitting beside her. "How much time do you figure we have left, Granny?"

"Ohh, I don't imagine too much more," she said while softly stroking the Child's hair. "We've done something special here, you know. We've been blessed with this very special experience. We must be thankful for the time we've been given together and not be greedy."

"I am thankful, Granny. This has been so wonderful. I'll treasure every moment." Then she straightened up and looked the old one in the eye. "I'll treasure every moment that I'm allowed to remember once I get back," she wisely revised.

The elder smiled as the Child slid off her lap.

"I get kinda heavy after a while," Little Self said, situating herself back on the bench seat. "Look," pointing down at the calico skirt, "I got it all wrinkled."

The old woman looked down as bid. "It's always wrinkled. And dirty. How nice and clean do you think these old skirts stay when I use them to hold the kindling I gather? Wrinkles? Wrinkles on the skirt, wrinkles on the face, whatever. They're nothing to me. But these wrinkles," she winked, looking down at her skirt, "these wrinkles are special because it was you who made them."

The little girl was touched, yet was uncomfortable with compliments. She used the subject matter to smartly slip into another subject. "Speaking of wrinkles, wasn't there some type of wrinkle to what we were last talking about? You know, about the Mother leaving out some of her planned titles?"

The gray brows knitted together. "I'm not sure what you mean."

"Well, you'd said that the *Sophia* book was the only one she didn't do, due to people's ignorance, how they twisted her words. Yet she also didn't finish the *Starborn* trilogy novels. Why'd she leave those out, if it wasn't due to the same thing?"

"Oh! Oh, now I see what you're getting at. She never finished the trilogy because she kept a close eye on the overall pulse of society. She observed a greater interest in 'alien' issues than in basic spirituality.

"It was a personal move on her part based on her determination of what was more needed in society. It was clear that people needed more spiritual behavioral philosophy, rather than the *Starborn* stuff they wanted. It came down to recognizing the difference between societal wants and needs. Simple. She chose the need."

The little one considered the answer. "So why didn't she take care of the needs and then society's wants?"

"Two reasons. One, she's not here for society's wants. Two, there wasn't enough time to get all those titles published."

"Not enough time?"

The elder shook her head. "That's what I said. She had to get her last title out and into people's hands by a certain date. So even if she did want to go ahead and write every title she had in mind to do, she wouldn't have had time unless she could publish two each year."

The small eyes widened with curiosity. "Why was there a time limit?"

"There just was," came the clipped response.

The Child tilted her head and gave her Granny a skeptical look. "Likely answer. I may be six years old, but my mind isn't."

"Ohh, don't I know it!" came the chuckled reply.

"Funny or not, it's true. Now, why was there a time limit on her writings?"

"Oh, stop being so suspicious. There was just a time for one phase of her purpose to end and another to begin."

"I'm not buying that, at least not completely. You gave me a bookend answer."

"A bookend answer?"

"Yeah, the beginning and the end. You left out what's in the middle."

"I did? You really think so?"

The small head bobbed with surety.

"The writing phase—the books—had to all be done before certain elements of the Changes began. There had to be a period of interim time between finishing the books and finishing the home preparations for certain upcoming events."

"That's what I thought you were going to say. It wasn't because she needed to get right to work on the humanitarian phase, it was because there was interim work to do between the two purposes."

After concurring with a nod, the old woman asked, "So,

does that answer all your questions on this now? Are you satisfied?"

"Ummm. I can think of more questions but I suppose I'm satisfied about the date thing. That means that the abbey and the women's shelter doesn't get going until some time later then."

"That's what it means."

"Can we go back to another issue?"

"We can go back to anything you please."

"When you said that the Mother did live by a lakeshore again, she eventually came back here."

"She did."

"But that's only a probability, right?"

"It is."

"So, she may alter that by deciding to remain by that lakeshore."

"She may."

Silence.

"Why? Why, Little Self, does that seem important to you?"

The small shoulders shrugged.

"Mmmm? You can tell me."

"Would you be mad at me if I wished she'd make that other choice when the time comes?"

"Which other choice?"

"To stay by the water."

"Why should I be mad? I'm wherever the Mother is—*we* are wherever she is. Makes no difference to me where we all end up." Then the old woman smiled. "Ohhh, I understand. *You* want to keep living by the water. Is that it?"

"Partly. Yes, I would like to go back and live by the water again and stay there, but that's not the only reason why I wish she'll make another choice about it. Mostly I wish it'll be different because of the harsh mountain winters here. Back in my time they're already getting harder on the Mother. I'd like to see her end up somewhere that's not so much work."

The Crone didn't understand the Child's logic. "I see little difference between the two places, honey. When she was back in Marquette, she needed winter firewood and had to shovel mountains of snow, too. Living on the shore of Lake Superior was very harsh during the winter months. And it was cold too! How is that any different?"

"I guess I was thinking of a smaller lake. Maybe one in a warmer state—as long as it's by the water."

"Little Self, you're forgetting the Changes and how they greatly altered the general climate world-over. You've come to visit me in autumntime. Perhaps if you'd come in the dead of winter you'd not found it so white and cold as it is back in your own time."

"It's warmer here now?"

"Absolutely. We still gather the firewood, but now we have the pleasure of doing it at our leisure because it's only used to take the chill out of the house once in awhile. We no longer need it for constant winter heat as we did in your time. Well," she admitted, "we also burn it more for the soothing aesthetics than for the need for warmth nowadays."

"Oh."

"Uh-huh. So, before you go wishing for alternate decisions to be made, you'd first better keep all related issues in mind."

The Child was thoughtful of those wise words of advice.

Grandma expanded. "There were a lot of dramatic changes between your time and mine, Little Self. And the probabilities both for them and those resulting from them were endless. You can't just wrap your hands around the stem of one plant and expect to yank it up without also disturbing a multitude of spreading roots hidden beneath."

The old woman's visual was a vivid conceptual picture for the youngster.

"I shouldn't have forgotten that. I hadn't thought about the change in world climate and everything else that will affect the geographic regions of my time. I went from A to Z without giving consideration to all the letters in between." She grinned. "I did bookend thinking."

The elder's voice was soft. "When we want the best for our loved ones we often do that, don't we?"

The Child nodded in agreement while listening to the other continue voicing her thoughts.

"For our loved ones, we want the very best to happen in a sudden manner—to magically manifest, poof!—without them having to go through the rigors of experiencing all the tribulations and heartbreaks it took to get there. Yet those same problems and troubles are just what makes a person stronger through the gaining of wise philosophical insights through those same personal life experiences."

"I know," sighed the little one, before jumping right into another question. "So . . . if the world's still here in your time, I guess it proved to a lot of people that the world didn't end like they thought it was going to."

"Well, it's certainly still here, that's for sure. Whether it ends tomorrow or four thousand years from now is anyone's guess. And that's exactly why we try to remember to live one day at a time, one blessed hour at a time. And that old belief in a physical Armageddon mostly just faded away after folks realized it was an individualized *Within* type of thing."

Little Self smiled and gazed down at her doll. She fussed a bit with its worn dress, smoothing it down and dusting off specks of dirt. Her face then lit up like a high alpine moon as it upturned to the elder beside her. "I like being a girl. I'm glad the Mother was a girl."

The old woman's hands flew up in the air and fell slapping down on her lap. "Ohh, what an odd thing to say! My, my, your little head is just spinning, isn't it? From Armageddon to being a girl! Whatever made you say that?"

"My feelings," came the answer through a widening grin. "I love my doll and my books and . . . well, you know, girl things."

The silvery brows shot down in a hard vee. "Boys have dolls. They call them 'action figures,' but we know they're still dolls to play with. Boys like books," she added. "Some boys even love their books. So! What is it about your doll and books that make them 'girl' things? And," she said, glancing down at the Child's patched knees of her coveralls, "don't I see you climbing trees all the time? Chasing after butterflies? Trying to catch frogs?"

"So?" Little Self defended. "Maybe I just didn't give good examples. Maybe I mean I like real girl things, like when the Mother wears lipstick and blush. I love walking along with her through the cosmetic section of the department store. I love it when she tests fragrances and sprays on perfume . . ."

"Little boys may love the scent of their father's cologne," the old one nonchalantly countered.

The small head tilted in suspicion, suspicion that the elder was coming back at her for a reason, yet full of determination to prove her point, she kept on. "I love the cedar incense she always burns at home and . . ."

"People put cedar in their clothes closets and linen chests to keep out moths."

"I love animals. I love my dogs."

"Ever read *Lassie Come Home* or *Old Yeller*?"

"Look!" said the Child as she shoved her hands beneath the elder's nose and stiffly splayed her fingers wide. "Nail polish! *Girl's* nail polish!"

The old one looked down at the pink-tipped fingernails. She noticed that the polish was worn and peeled. She took the fingers in her hands and rubbed the nails with both thumbs. "Nail polish. Mmmm. I think you got me on that one."

The Child beamed.

"But what are we talking about here, Little Self? What are we really talking about?"

"About how much I love being a girl!"

"Are we?"

"Yes!"

"You're sure?"

"YES!"

"Aren't we really talking about liking the basic who of you?"

"Yes, and I'm a *girl*!"

"Girl or boy, Little Self, it matters not. The basic, underlying fact is that you very much like who you are."

The Child frowned as she thought on that.

"You see," the Crone softly explained, "it doesn't matter what gender you are as long as you like yourself, as long as you truly like and enjoy being who you are. If the Mother had been male you would've likewise loved being a little boy. You would've loved doing boy things and enjoyed being near the man things the Father did and used."

With that the Child vehemently shook her head. "No! No, I wouldn't!"

"You don't know that, Little Self. You can't know that."

"But I do! I do know! Besides," she smoothly slipped in, "men don't have a trined consciousness."

"That wasn't fair play, Little Self. Everyone has a Higher Self. Everyone has a Child Within. What else explains some men's fascination with their boyhood things? Some adult men have elaborate train sets built over many tables in their basements. Don't you think that relates to their Child Within?"

"No. It just shows that they have a high interest in trains. Maybe they were a train conductor in their last life or something like that."

"That's true. That could very well be the reasoning behind such an adulthood fascination, yet whether you want to admit it or not the fact remains that everyone walking this planet possesses a Child Within."

"It's not the same, Granny! History isn't full of legends of a man's Child/Father/Wiseman myth! Phuugh," she puffed indignantly, "no one's ever heard of that!"

"That's true, too. It's also true that it's not the same, that the elementary, singular concept cannot be exactly applied to both genders because it's clear that they aren't the same when one attempts to do so—to make the concept fit a male host. However, males still have a Higher Self and a Child Within."

The youngster knew she'd been bested. She whispered, "We were talking about me liking being a girl."

"Yes, we were. And it's good that you like being the girl you are. That means you like the who of you." Weathered fingers reached out to lift up the little chin. "Mmm?"

Though the younger one knew that the other was right, philosophically, she also felt that she'd gotten her own point of view across. She raised her eyes to lock on the elder's. "Yeah, I like the who of me. I like being who I am." Then she added one for the road, just for the fun of it. "I really like being a girl."

A sigh escaped from the old woman as she rolled her eyes up to the heavens. "Do you also really like having the last word?"

"No," the Child innocently declared. "I just like to make my thoughts clear, that's all. I understood what you had to say and I just wanted to say that I also still have my own feelings about it. I guess I have two views of it now—yours and also my own."

"I never meant to change your view, Little Self, only to expand them, only to widen them."

"Sure, that's okay," the Child shrugged. "I know what you meant to do." She grinned then. "That's kinda your job, isn't it?"

The smile was returned. "You could say that. It just comes naturally after so many years of doing it."

"And I'm just doing my job. I'm being a six-year-old who wants to know all the how's and why's to absolutely everything."

The old woman huffed with cynical amusement. "Oh, right, a six-year-old with the mind of an old crone hidden in it."

With that Little Self filled the garden with childlike laughter. A sound that rang out as a song, a song the garden hadn't heard in a very long time.

Chapter Sixteen

Groaning, the elder stood and rubbed her backside. "Don't have the padding I used to have," she chuckled. "These benches look nice, but they're sure not conducive to prolonged sitting."

Standing too, the Child replied, "You need some of those nice chair cushions on them. Then you could sit longer in your garden."

The old one brushed away the idea with a wave of her hand. "I put chair and bench cushions out here and, within a week, they'll be full of holes. Chippers will nab the insides to line their nests."

"Oh, yeah, I forgot about them. The Mother puts her vacuum bag dust, dog brush leavings, and dryer lint out for the critters to use. The birds and chippers eventually take it all away. Rabbits, too, sometimes. Nothing much goes to waste around the house."

"We still do those things," Grandma assured. "But leaving a nice bench cushion out all the time would be too much temptation for those chippers. Besides, I usually don't sit out here for that long a time."

"Want to walk along the garden paths?" asked the small one.

"Sure, we can do that if you like."

Little Self made sure she took her Raggedy Ann along with her. The doll dangled as the Child held onto the end of one cottony hand.

Strolling about, they came upon a four-foot statue and stopped before it. It stood tall among the multi-colored autumn chrysanthemums growing in profusion around its feet.

"That looks American Indian," commented the Child while tilting her head, "but I don't think it really is."

"You're right, it's not. It's a replica of a Frank Lloyd Wright sculpture called 'Garden Sprite.' It's a bit unusual in design. Do you like it?"

Eyeing the piece with indecision, Little Self tossed her head this way and that. "Mmm, I think so. I think it's one of those things that you have to get used to, though. I like the unusual style of it. It's called . . . ummm, it's called. What's it called? That style?"

"Art deco. Sally saw this garden piece in a catalog and so the Mother gave it to her one year as a Christmas gift."

"Mmmm, well, yes," Little Self finally decided, "I do like it."

"It's okay with me if you truly don't, you know. You won't hurt my feelings. The art deco style doesn't appeal to everyone's taste."

"I know, but honestly, I do like it. I'd be honest with you. I'd tell you if I didn't care for it."

"Yes, knowing you, you most likely wouldn't mince words over it."

They both stood looking at the odd, yet interesting, statuary and the old woman took the opportunity to expand on the subject of the novelty of both its design and architect.

"Mr. Wright was a maverick in his time. He had vision unlike any other architect. That vision evidenced itself in his unparalleled and innovative building designs." The Crone frowned. "He was not readily accepted among his peers nor the public. He was ridiculed and shunned for his unique and wildly diverse visions."

That reminded the girl of something. "I once read a book . . . well, I read it along with the Mother when she was reading it. It was about an architect just like that. Mmmm. Know what?"

"What?"

"I think Ayn Rand had someone special in mind when she wrote *The Fountainhead*."

"You do, do you?"

"Yep," nodded the Child with conviction. "I think she was writing about Frank Lloyd Wright."

"And how did you come to this hypothesis? Did you glean it from the Mother's thoughts while she was reading it?"

"Well," came the sheepish reply given in half-hidden admission, "the same idea may have passed through her mind, too. She thought of Mr. Wright quite a lot while reading."

"Even so, Little Self, what's the point? What's the point of speculating about who the book is about rather than what it's about?"

The Child's face scrunched up. "What? What it's about?"

"Why, yes. Isn't it all about innovative ideas and indi- vidualized visions?"

"Uh-huh."

"Well, there you have it."

"Have what?"

"Philosophy. Spiritual philosophy."

"You lost me."

The old woman chuckled. "No, I didn't. You're still right here."

Little Self rolled her eyes. "Okay . . . if you say so."

"No! Never just because I or anyone says so, but because it's true!"

"Well, yes, I know that," said the Child while still trying to sort out the conversation. Then, "Oh yes! I get it! Now I get it! Tolerance! You're talking about having tolerance of other people's ideas, opinions, and visions!"

"Of course, I am, and so were you. Difference is, you just didn't realize what you were actually talking about. Now you do."

The little one let out a humph of realization. She then grinned up at her friend. "You're doing it again, you know. You've turned a conversation about something into a lesson."

"Nooo," Granny exclaimed in a voice heavy with dramatized aghast. And immediately a reciprocal smile deepened the laugh lines on the woman's face. "I have? Would I do that?"

"Do birds sing in the woods?"

"Birds sing almost everywhere," came the response that was given too quickly before the speaker realized she'd snagged herself in the little one's clever trap.

"Precisely," finalized the young one with a slight hint of childlike snugness in her tone. "See what I mean? They sing almost everywhere, any time. Just like you, just like how you sing out your lessons at every opportunity." The Child then reached out a hand to gently grasp the elder's. "That's all right, Granny, that's what you're supposed to do. Just like the birds are supposed to make people feel good with their singing and chirping, you make people feel good with new thoughts—deeper thoughts."

"Why, thank you for that. You made a fine analogy. Although I think you may have overstated my effectiveness. My habit of making people think doesn't always go over so well. It doesn't always make people feel good to have to apply deeper thought to things. Even so, I thank you for your kindness."

The Child squeezed the other's hand. "You're very welcome. So!" she piped. "Are we going to talk about tolerance then?"

"We don't have to. Whatever you like, Honey. We can talk about whatever you like."

Little Self glanced at the statue. "I don't really need to discuss all the aspects of tolerance, but there is one thing I would like to know about it."

"And what's that?"

"After all this time has passed since my time and yours, has society become more tolerant of people's differences?"

"That seems to be important to you. Why?"

"Because back in my time people aren't at all tolerant of each other. There's a lot of hate going on. A lot of hate crimes happening. Prejudice and personal superiority is so common that I wondered if it'd improved since then? I wondered because that's one of the things I really want to see changed in society, not only because it would make a better world, but mostly because the Mother's made it one of her most important messages."

The elder reached over and patted their tightly-clasped hands. "That's a wonderful thing to wish for, Little Self."

The Child didn't like the hidden tone of that comment. "A wish? Is that what it is . . . was? Only a wish?"

"Now don't jump to conclusions. I never said that it was only wishful thinking on your part, did I now?"

"No, but . . ."

"Hmmm?"

"No, but your tone of voice implied that it was wishful thinking."

"Watch yourself now. Mustn't read so much into some-one's tone of voice. Sometimes tone of voice reveals much, other times, nothing at all and then misconceptions are falsely assumed from that single error in judgement. Be careful, Little Self. Take the spoken words at face value instead of reading additional elements into them."

"Okay, so can I conclude that it wasn't wishful thinking then? That people did learn tolerance for each other after all this time?"

"That's still an assumption. The people learned to have more tolerance for the differences of others. And, if you think about it, Honey, that's still a good thing. Tolerance is gaining ground in society."

"But why hasn't it gained more ground, Granny? I would've thought that after so many years and after every-thing that happened to people during the Changes they would've learned to pull together and realize that every-one's in it together for the long haul."

"Many have realized that, yet remember, everyone has an ego. Many have learned to successfully integrate that personal ego with all societal aspects of their lives. Yet there are still those who have not learned this all-important lesson. Those people still view themselves with a percep-tion of specialness, of a specialness or special beingness— one above and superior to others.

"Little Self," the Crone reminded, "there will always be those who think themselves better than others. There will always be those who think their gender, philosophical or political belief system, lifestyle, religion, ethnicity, etc., is superior to others."

Little Self stamped her foot. "But, why?"

"Because the sense of personal ego—the Self—is too strong in them for the intellectual wisdom of their mind to override."

The Child made a frown. "You make it sound like a habit, an addiction."

"Mmmm, that's an interesting thing to say. That's a very interesting analogy. Actually, you're not far off the mark with it. Having a sense of ego that is stronger than the mind's intellect can indeed be likened to having an addiction to the Self. Today there are still people with that type of addiction."

"I'm sorry to hear that," Little Self mumbled.

"Why? You're seeing the glass half-empty instead of half-full! Didn't I just say that there's *more* tolerance in the world now?"

The young one nodded without much enthusiasm.

"Yes," she reticently admitted beneath her breath.

Grandma vigorously shook their clasped hands for encouragement. "Oh, for heaven's sake, c'mon! Open your eyes to the new lights shining from society instead of letting your sights be drawn to the few shadows they cast."

Little Self looked up into the elder's face. A half-smile upturned the corners of her mouth. "I guess some improvement is better than none," she finally admitted. "I'd been in expectation about things being better than that—a lot better—after all this time," she said, pausing before finishing her thoughts. "Changes come at a turtle's pace, don't they, Granny?"

"Most do, Child. Most do."

"They come about very, very slowly," she said thoughtfully. "People's new ideas, like inventions and advances in technology seem to come about pretty fast, yet their behavior and perspective drags way behind."

"Mmmm."

"I mean, it's almost like people are letting their brains pull them along while their souls are being dragged behind them like unwanted luggage."

The Crone was impressed. "Do you think their souls and the soul's spiritual philosophy is secondary, like an afterthought to people's lives?"

"I think many people perceive the living of right spiritual philosophy as being a drag on them. I think many people view it as baggage they have to lug along behind them. They act like it's a big pain in the butt that they have to give attention to right behavior instead of just going ahead and doing whatever they want."

"Some folks feel and act that way. That's because they choose to let the ego rule their lives. The trick is to let their soul rule everything they do."

"Those kinds of people have things backwards, huh, Granny."

"Huh, Little Self."

Chapter Seventeen

The old one gave the young one a comforting smile as they both turned as one from the statue that stood in protective guard over the work of the flower devas.

Following along the flagstone path, the Child came up with another brand new question. "Granny?" she began in her usual way.

"Yesss?" sang the Crone.

"Is it ever okay to tell a lie?"

Silence.

Waiting.

"What's your opinion, Little Self?"

"I asked you first."

"I know, but first I'd like you to share your own opinion."

Without a moment's hesitation or the slightest sign of self-doubt, the Child said with complete assurance, "I think, yes."

The old woman didn't immediately respond.

The youngster leaned forward to look up into Grandma's face which held no visible clue as to her reaction.

"Well?" Little Self pushed. "I told you my opinion, now what do you think?"

"I wouldn't disagree," came the concurring reply.

That made the small one's eyes brighten with satisfaction. "That's one of those funny 'exception to the rule' things, isn't it, Granny."

"Yes, it is, although many people would disagree."

"They'd be wrong, though."

"Wrong? They just wouldn't have thought it through, because there are various reasons why a lie would not be wrong to voice." Curiously, the Crone glanced down at the girl. "What prompted this question? Were you thinking of some specific lie told?"

"Not really," she said in an unconvincing tone while letting go of Grandma's hand. Turning around, Little Self skipped backwards in front of her.

"This path's not straight," cautioned the elder. "You'd better turn back around before you run into something."

The Child promptly did as suggested and grasped the other's hand again. She held up her doll. "Want to hold her for awhile?"

"Would you like me to?"

"Sure, but only if you wanna."

"I wanna," Grandma said, opening her hand to receive Raggedy Ann. She gave it a long gaze before bringing it next to her heart as they strolled the stone walkway. "So. We were talking about the fact that there're good reasons to lie sometimes. Something tells me you have one or two appropriate examples in mind."

"The Mother had to lie sometimes," the Child quickly piped up.

The elder thought back. "I recall some of those instances."

"But those were okay," chirped Little Self. "They were okay lies because they kept an old woman from starving or hurting herself."

Granny grinned. "That end certainly justified the means, didn't it?"

"Of course! When the Mother and Sally were taking care of Sally's mother, Mary Belle, they had to lie a lot. They had to tell Mary Belle lies to get her to eat her food and to take her medicine. Sally's mother tried to do things to end her life like starving herself and refusing medication. Their lies kept her eating. They got the medication down. When she refused food they'd tell her that they were going to put her in the hospital, where a feeding tube would be used to get nutrients into her. They told her that because they knew Mary Belle didn't want to go back to a hospital anymore. Their little white lies kept her health up."

"So it was using psychology, wasn't it?"

"Yes, psychology that was still a lie though," clarified the Child.

"So you think it was justified because it kept an old woman from starving herself to death or missing her daily medications?"

"Sure. Sure I do."

"Me, too," the Crone said with a wink. "Those are good examples of not taking the letter of the law too seriously. Many times the 'end' of something has to be given very serious consideration before a behavioral decision is made and then acted on. Placing the means and the end on a spiritual scale is a good practice to get into the habit of doing. Telling a lie to an old woman so she'll take her medication is a balanced act. It's the end result—positive or negative— that makes a lie the determining factor as to whether or not it's wrong."

The Child rolled her eyes. "Trouble is, some people don't know the difference or else they rationalize or color that end result to fit their needs."

"Sometimes. Sometimes they tend to make false justifications for their wrong behavior. People have to closely watch their motives for doing the things they do, whether it's a lie or some other type of behavior. The motive behind a lie can either tip the scale or keep it balanced in a level position."

"Yeah, the motive. Motives are important for people to watch. They have to be really honest when looking at them, huh."

"That's a given, Little Self. That's a given."

The two had strolled to a section of the garden where nothing grew.

"What's all this dirt?" asked the Child.

"That's what's left of the summer vegetables. We ate them! We ate some and gave some away to friends."

"What'd you grow?"

"This was the section where we grew green onions and chives. Mmmm," Grandma groaned with remembered pleasure, "they were the best green onions we'd ever tasted. They grew big and tall, too!"

"The Mother grows those," added the Child. "She goes out in the garden and cuts fresh chives and green onions for their morning omelets and dinner salads."

"I know. And, as you can see, we've expanded the garden quite a bit since your time. There's not a lot of vegetables we can grow at this elevation and, after some trial and error, we've managed to add a few more varieties along the way. We've also managed to do quite well with the greenhouse we built," she said, nodding toward a small building on a sunny rise outside the garden fencing. "Some of our friends helped us put it together and we've been able to extend the growing season. It's been wonderful, something more for us to putter around with while we're growing old."

"What about the chippers, Granny? And the bunnies? Don't you have trouble with them gobbling everything up?"

"Just like the Mother does, I still sprinkle powdered garlic over the soil." The Crone looked down at the Child and grimaced. "Those chippers don't care for garlic. Didn't back then, don't now. It still works. Same in the flower section of the gardens, under the lilacs, too. Works great and it's natural to boot."

Little Self looked back down at the tilled mulch of the greenless patch. "It's an awful lot of work," she commented with concern in her voice. "You've added so much. It's not too much work now, is it, Granny?"

"Oh, my no! What else do old women like us have to do with all their time?"

The small shoulders hunched up and dropped down. "I dunno."

"Ahhh," the Crone happily sighed, rotating her shoulders. "Keeps the old joints oiled nicely. All that digging, planting, pruning, and harvesting." She winked. "Keeps me from turning into a mummy!"

The infectious laughter of a child rang out and filled the garden like the fragrant scent of sweetly, blooming spring flowers. "That's funny! I could never envision you as an old, dried-up mummy! Oh, Granny, that's too silly!"

"Is it, now. Child, time marches on. It stops for no one. No indeed, no one escapes the effects of time."

Little Self's brow arched teasingly in exaggerated question. "Oh, really?"

"Well. Time hasn't really stopped for us, has it, Dear? It's more that we're caught up in that very special twilight time. In reality, nobody escapes the movements of nature's perpetual gears as each cog clicks down into place, one after the other. Time catches up with us all—every last one of us."

"The Mother's getting old," said the Child.

"You don't say."

"Yeah," she sighed. "Sometimes she catches glimpses of you looking back at her from the mirror."

"Really!"

The little one made a face. "Guess you already know that, huh."

Wispy hairs on the old woman's head wafted in the magical light of twilight as she nodded. "Yesss. Oh, yes, I know that. She's getting glimpses of what she'll one day become, glimpses of herself as an old woman. I suppose you could say that that reflection she sees is the Crone of herself. That wouldn't be beyond reason or stretching it." Smiling down at the youngster, Grandma added, "I also noticed that she doesn't mind seeing herself as being old."

"Nope!" Little Self proudly zipped back. "She thinks growing old is sorta nice."

"Nice?"

"Nice," the Child repeated. "I mean, she doesn't mind it at all like some women would. The changes in her looks are accepted, only . . ."

"Only? Only what?"

Little Self cupped her hand to her mouth as if to reveal a secret. She whispered, "She doesn't care for the gray in her hair."

"I thought you just said that she's looking forward to growing old? If she doesn't like the gray in her hair, doesn't that sound a bit contradictory?"

"No, no, no, you don't get it. It's not, really. What she doesn't like is the salt 'n' pepper look. She wants it to hurry up and be *all* silver."

"Oh, dear, well! That makes a difference. That definitely changes the look of things."

The Child put her hand over her mouth to hide a smirking grin. "You just made a pun!"

Thinking about what she'd just said, the old woman smirked back. "I guess I did."

"Anyway," Little Self said, "I'm glad she's not afraid to grow old."

Silence.

The Child began humming.

"Why do you think that is?" asked the Crone.

The little tune stopped. "Why what is, Granny?"

"Why the Mother isn't afraid to grow old, to look like an old woman?"

Little Self flashed a look of exasperation over at the elder for not realizing how obvious the answer was. "It's because she likes being a *girl* and, being a granny is part of being a girl, silly!"

The old woman's silver eyebrows shot upward. "Why, Little Self!" she spouted. "You little monkey, you are one stubborn child! You wormed your way right back to that 'girl' thing again!"

The young one, filled with mischief, effervescently giggled like a woodland pixie caught in the act of pulling a prank. "I'm sorry, I was just teasing you. The Mother doesn't mind growing old because she's comfortable with her beingness . . . she likes the Who of herself."

"That's more like it! My goodness, you sure can be impish sometimes."

The elder was greeted with a playful puckish grin. "I know."

Grandma played back. She feigned sternness while bending down and getting nose-to-nose with her small companion. She made a great show of examining the little face in a dramatically scrutinizing manner.

"What?" asked the self-conscious Child. "What! What're you doing?"

The elder remained noncommittal as she gently ran her fingers over the tips of the Child's ears.

"Stop that!" giggled the Child, gently swatting at Granny's hands. "If you're looking for dirt in my ears, I don't have any."

The old woman paid no mind to the youngster's concealed irritation. "Mmmm," she mumbled, while digging out her granny glasses from her voluminous skirt pocket. Setting them down on just the right spot of her nose, she more closely examined the small earlobes.

"Granny," Little Self spouted with a touch of forced patience in her voice, "what're you doing? What're you looking for?"

"Mmmm?"

"I said, what are you doing? What're you looking for?"

Grandma pulled back. She squinted to eye the Child. "Do I detect impatience? Are you getting impatient with me? Is that what you're doing?"

"No," came the big white lie. "I just want to know what you're looking for in my ears."

Again the glasses were adjusted as the old one bent down and, as if holding a sorceress' magic wand, tapped an earlobe. "Points," she nonchalantly whispered.

The Child burst out laughing. She never laughed so hard in her life. "Points! You pulled a good one, Granny!"

Smiling wide with eyes all atwinkle, Granny laughed back. With her hands on her hips she exclaimed, "Well! Whatever was I to think? The way you behave sometimes makes me think that you're wearing a Halloween costume, a 'little girl' costume over that elfin body of yours!" Grandma leaned down to get nose-to-nose with the Child. "I was sure you had pointed ears hidden behind all that hair!"

Still caught in the initial fit of wild laughter, the Child skipped and romped around the flagstones. Eyes dancing and arms flinging about in abandoned merriment, she was the picture of childlike joy.

The Crone's shirt billowed out as she joined in and twirled while keeping her eye on the circling elf prancing around her. She instigated deeper laughter by saying, "Look at you! You're a fairy child!"

Hearing that, the elf stopped. She ran to the old woman and wrapped her small arms about the narrow waist and buried her head in the soft folds of the long skirt. "I love you, Granny. Oh, I love you so much! You're so funny. You're so much fun to be with. I want to stay here forever!"

Long arms covered the Child's back and wrinkled hands tenderly stroked the denim overall fabric. "I love you, too, Little Self." She sighed and looked high up into the twilight sky. "I surely do love you. But I don't think you meant that last part, not really."

The Child glanced up and locked eyes with Grandma. "I do mean it. I mean, I want to be in both places."

"Only one time frame can be lived at a time. You belong back with the Mother in the present. We're still together there, we're still together there in her consciousness." Then she frowned. "What, she's no fun? Is that it?"

"No," came the somewhat deflated reply. "It's not that." Then, "Well . . ."

"She's walking over some rough spots in the road right now. What with helping to care for Sally's mother and trying to finish up her books. She's got a plateful to handle all at once. Things may not be as rosy and light-hearted as you'd like them to be, but they'll improve, they'll improve. I promise they will. Besides, grandmas are supposed to be fun to be with, not like the mothers who are so very busy all the time."

A long sigh escaped from the Child's lips. "I guess it's that old 'skipping from A to Z' thing again. I want things in the Mother's life to hurry up and be at a certain stage—a certain time in the future—where things are going more smoothly and, well . . . more normal. Like, well, like I want the time to arrive when she and Sally can actually rent that little shop they've had their eyes on. It's not fair when the Mother gets those premonition visions of it being their gift shop-of-the-future. She sees the exact color they paint the outside of it and the gold lettering of their business name on the window. She sees it being busy with customers and sees Sally demonstrating to people how the metal sculpture is created. It's such a cool vision of the future and . . . and right now she has to drive by that old building and live with those future visions—wanting very badly for it to be a reality . . . now." Little Self then became animated. Arms flung out. "I don't think it's fair to have nice visions of 'Z'—of the future—while still being caught living in 'C'—a time when that vision is still an impossibility for her to achieve." She stomped her foot in frustration. "I think that's terribly unfair! It's not only unfair, it's plain mean!"

"R," came the singular, cryptic reply.

The animations froze in mid-air. "What?"

"R," the old one calmly repeated.

"R?"

"Yes," Grandma nodded. "The time frame for the manifestation of that particular vision. The Mother's currently living around the 'R' position of your alphabet timeline."

"R?"

Again the wispy silver hairs wafted with the nod. "That's what I said. So see? It's really not so far away, that vision she gets."

"Still . . . still I think it's unfair."

"But is it, Little Self? Is it really?"

The Child reached for the other's hand.

They turned to continue strolling along the flagstone walkway that led through the autumn gardens.

"Little Self," Grandma gently began, "don't you think

those visions the Mother has of her future are meaningful? Very meaningful for her?"

"Sure," the Child replied dejectedly, "they force her to live in acceptance of being helpless to make them come about now. They only say, 'Wait! Wait! Wait!' They're frustrating, that's what they are."

"Frustrating to whom?"

The Child deliberately chose not to respond.

"Frustration comes from not having acceptance for What Is. Frustration comes from not wanting to wait for That Which Will Be."

"Can you blame her for not wanting to have to wait?"

"No. I think that's natural, yet it causes anxiety and that's not good. Anxiety causes emotional and mental stress. Those end up showing up as physical ills."

The Child suddenly became defensive of the Mother. "Are you saying that she doesn't have enough acceptance for What Is?"

The elder frowned. "Wait a minute. Wait just one minute. Weren't *you* the one who said something about 'being forced to have acceptance'? Do you think she's having some trouble with acceptance over having to wait for the time for that shop to manifest?"

The long braids bobbed in answer. "Nobody's perfect," she mumbled beneath her breath.

"That's true, yet that's not the final word on this. It goes much deeper, her feelings. Those feelings of deep anxiety for the time for that shop to manifest entails a great many related elements. Those elements are connected to the Changes. That cutesie little shop represents a new beginning after the geologic Changes!"

The Child's eyes widened. "Ohhh, I get it. It's not just a matter of not dealing well with needing to have acceptance for the wait, it's more of wanting the worst of the Changes to be over and done with. That vision represents the time when the world will have gotten back to a more normal and stabilized state!"

"Yes! You see? It represents a societal state stabilized enough to maintain successful commerce once again. Oh, yes, Little Self," the old woman lightly chuckled, "that attractive, little forest green storefront with the metallic gold lettering represents a great deal more than just a simple personal craft shop—it represents a great deal more."

"No wonder she has tinges of anxiety and feels a little impatient whenever she gets that vision. No wonder she has pangs of longing every time she drives past it."

"Mmmm."

The Child was deep in thought. "But, Granny, isn't it still unfair?"

"As to what? How so?"

"To have clear visions of 'Z' when you're living in 'R' and can't do anything about it yet?"

"Those premonition visions have their upside, Dear. There's always an upside to those special things."

The Child was doubtful. "Could've fooled me."

"Really. I haven't seen a whole lot of evidence of much fooling you in life. I've been watching. I know. You're sharper than you think you are, especially when you don't want to admit that fact."

"What's that supposed to mean?"

"Just what you think it does."

"I'm not fooling myself. I don't see any upside to the Mother's vision of their future shop. All it does is make her heart yearn for it, especially now when she needs something happy and good to look forward to."

Silence.

The Child then realized she'd just fallen into a net of her

own weaving. She sighed with the knowledge, yet didn't immediately feel the urge to voice her discovery.

Neither did the old woman walking beside her.

Finally Little Self was ready to conclude the issue. "Hope," she whispered. "That vision of the little shop not only represents the Mother's future, it symbolizes hope."

The Crone smiled warmly. "Hope and?" she gently prompted.

"Hope and . . . and ummm. Hope and . . . I dunno."

"Reassurance," came the encouraging reply. "Even more than hope it gives reassurance—a verification—that life will resume beyond the Changes. You could almost say that that reassurance negates the necessity for hope because it reveals a surety for the world's future." The old woman looked down at the Child. "Did you understand that?"

"Yes. Hope is for when you don't know the future—for when there are no clear visions of it or how it will be. Hope fades, it isn't necessary when one does have a clear vision of the future. The clear vision supplies the reassurance that replaces the hope caused by the unknown. Hope is for the unknown. Reassurance is for the known."

The Crone's chest puffed up with pride in the Child's fine mind. "That pretty well explains it, Little Self. Couldn't have summed it better myself. See there? See what a wonderful upside comes with the Mother's vision?"

"Yesss . . ."

"But?"

"But, I'm not sure she's looking at it quite like that."

"Oh, she is. Believe me, she is! Otherwise she wouldn't be so antsy to have it finally become a reality."

"It's still hard waiting for it," insisted the Child. "It's still hard having to accept that dumb waiting stuff."

"Ahhh, yes, the waiting. The waiting is what makes the

getting so much sweeter." She gave the small hand a quick squeeze for emphasis. "You'll see. Just wait, Honey. You'll see I'm right."

Little Self gave Grandma a genuine smile. "You usually are, Granny. You usually are. Thank you for helping me with this. I just hate it every time we drive by that old, paint-peeling building and see that vision come before her mind." She tugged her friend's hand and smiled wide. "When it does happen it's going to be sooo pretty. They're going to fix it all up in a really, really neat old fashioned way. And know what? Know what else?"

"What?"

"I think that, eventually, the Mother's readers will realize that, besides the abbey, the shop will be the only other place that they can indirectly connect with her. They'll like that, won't they?"

"Oh, yes, they'll like that very much. They'll very much like having some little ornamental thing that she helped make."

The small one tilted her head. "In my time she's already helping Sally make things down in their basement workshop. A couple local gift shops put them in their stores. She came up with an idea for single brass aspen leaf Christmas tree ornament and they ended up being pretty popular with people. I especially like the long-stemmed, red copper roses Sally makes. One shop customer ordered two gross of them!"

"I know, that was a nice surprise, wasn't it?"

Little Self nodded in great satisfaction. Amusingly, she began sounding like a seasoned entrepreneur. "It takes a while for word to get around," she informed. "It takes some time to get something like that going."

"Yes, it does, Little Self, it surely does. Just keep the vision of that future shop strong. Be glad of it because it proves that their project gets more than going . . . it takes off!"

With that, the Child beamed like the evening star in a clear, alpine night. She was finally satisfied that all the Mother's time spent between "R" and "Z" was time that would be well worth the wait.

Chapter Eighteen

Their footfalls brought them to the low stone wall that bordered the mature lilac.

Like minds shared the same idea as they both seated themselves.

A light breeze carried spent leaves sprinkling down on them.

The Child caught one in her hand before it fell to ground. "You called me a fairy child," she reminded.

"Mmmm, only because your behavior, your mannerisms, and innocence remind me of one sometimes."

That idea tickled Little Self's insides. "They do?"

"They do."

"I spied a fairy once," the Child said, sharing her secret. "It was a long time ago, though. We—the Mother, I mean—would like to get a picture of one someday." Little Self cocked her head up at her companion. "Do you think that that'll ever happen? I'm not sure it's even possible to get a fairy on film. What do you think?"

"Ohhh, I think it's all possible. That's the primal reality of life, is it not? Possibilities. Sure, it's possible that you'll spy one or more again, and it's possible to get them on film. Just depends, is all."

"On what, Granny? On what does it depend?"

"On if they want to be seen and if they wish their personal images imprinted on film." The old one raised a cautioning finger. "They know how someone is planning on using that film. Oh, yes, they know. Indeed they do!"

"Oh," was all the little one said on the subject as she cast her gaze up into the backlighted evergreen branches. After a time, she said, "The owl's gone."

The Crone looked to the tree. "She'll be back. That spot seems to be one of her favorite hangouts."

"I don't hear the nighthawk anymore. It must've flown away too."

"Must have."

No sounds came except the hushed wind brushing through the shadowy high pines and spruces.

"Why?" the grandmother asked.

"Huh? Why what?"

"Why'd you ask about the fairies?"

"Oh, I don't know," came the sheepish reply.

The elder bent far forward and peeked around into the young one's downcast face. "You don't know? I hardly think so."

The Child's eyes slid up to meet her companion's. "I think you know what I'm getting at. I just feel sorta like I'm taking advantage of you, of your future time, to keep asking so many questions. I don't mean to be bugging you so much about things."

Grandma's hand patted one overall-covered knee as she made a dismissive hand gesture to blow off the statement. "Phooey! We're here together like this, so we can talk about whatever we want. Whatever," she emphasized before softening her tone. "Don't do that to yourself, Child. Don't go guilt-tripping yourself over all those questions tumbling around in your mind. That's just plain natural, especially for such a curious child as yourself. I don't mind one bit."

This brought a curling grin to the formerly solemn countenance. "Okay," chirped the quick response. "I was wondering if the Mother ever did get her photograph?"

"Ahhh, so that's what this is about."

The Child didn't buy that contrived attitude of innocence. She stuck out a small finger and waved it at the old one. "You knew," she wagged in a knowing tone. "You knew all along where I was going with my question."

"Though it did seem obvious I didn't want to assume anything I shouldn't."

"Okay," the Child decided with pursed lips. "I'll accept that excuse."

"Excuse! That was no excuse, it was my reason! There's a difference!"

Grinning, "I accept your reason, then. So," she prompted, looking for her answer.

"So?"

Little Self jumped off the stone wall. In animated exasperation she stood directly in front of the old woman and dramatically planted her hands on her hips. "So . . . ? Did she ever get her picture of a fairy?"

Grandma's eyes danced and her hands clapped together. "Yes!"

Hearing the wished-for answer, the Child whooped, "Yessss!" as she hopped about in explosive glee. "YES!" she sang to the sky. "Oh, YES!" Then, unable to contain her joy, she threw her arms around Grandma. "Oh, I'm so happy! I'm so happy about that!"

Hugging the exuberant youngster back, Grandma couldn't avoid being affected by the contagious emotion. She felt as though she were trying to hold onto a flitting firefly. She laughed heartily. "My goodness, Child, you're actually trembling!"

Little Self released her grip from around the old body

and solemnly looked deep into the aged eyes. Intently, she peered back and forth into each glistening orb. Placing a palm on each side of the creviced cheeks, she tenderly cradled the Crone's face and softly whispered. "I love you, Granny. I love you so."

As the old woman's eyes began to sting with welling emotion, she raised a hand to tenderly stroke the side of the Child's face. The knobby blue veins of the time-worn hand contrasted sharply to the Child's smooth and youthful tawny skin. The elder's words came haltingly. "Oh, Little Self, you've . . . you've touched places in . . . in my heart that have too long been . . . forgotten. Those soft spots have . . . I, I . . . I don't know how to . . . ."

Not wanting to cause the old one an ounce of sadness, the Child quickly put a finger up to the woman's quivering lips and smiled sweetly. "Shhhh, now," she hushed, "shhhhh." Then, acting as though she was about to share a huge secret, she inched her nose so close to the old one's, they touched. In a sweetly soft voice, the Child whispered, "A puppy can touch those heart spots, too."

That was just too much sensitivity to bare. Granny reached out and cradled the Child's head to her bodice. She held tight and slowly rocked them both back and forth. Instead of the misting tears being forced back, the little one's words had acted like the pull of the moon on the old one's heart.

The tears were magnetically drawn like the tide waters and finally brimmed to their flood stage level.

They crested and freely spilled forth.

Flowing in rivulets that coursed along time-worn patterns down the weathered face, the old woman whispered back, "Oh-h-h yes-s-s, Child, I know. I know."

Chapter Nineteen

A hard lump was suddenly lodged in the little girl's throat. She eased herself away from grandma's chest. Pulling the frayed cuff of her flannel shirt down over her palm, she carefully wiped away the wetness on the creviced cheeks. Dabbing gently around the old woman's blinking eyes, she swallowed hard. Then, flashing a star-bright smile, she chimed, "That's why you need one! That's why you need a puppy!"

The elder chortled, "You're not going to give up, are you, Honey?"

"Nope," Little Self laughed.

The Crone sighed. "I know what you're saying," she admitted before starting to huff and fuss about herself. "Good gracious," she exclaimed with a nervous chuckle, while wiping at her face and patting her hair, "old women sure can get weepy, sometimes, can't they?"

Little Self stood before Granny. Resting her palms on both knees of the calico skirt, she said, "Weepy, mushy, tearful, what's the difference? They all come from here," she whispered, placing a small hand on the Crone's chest. "From the heart. I think you didn't realize how much you miss having a puppy."

"Oh. Is that what you think?"

"Yep."

The old one eyed her. "Maybe it had nothing at all to do with a puppy. Maybe it had to do with you and you just don't want to admit it."

The Child eyed her back. "Maybe it had to do with a puppy and you don't want to admit that."

"Know what?" Grandma smiled.

"What?"

"Maybe we're both right. Do you think that that's a possibility?"

"Mmmm," hummed the Child as she thoughtfully put finger-to-chin to mull it over. "Uh-huh, I think that's a good possibility."

Little Self hopped back on the stone wall and settled herself beside her granny. Eyes scanning the deep woods surrounding the cottage, she listened for the telltale sounds of nature critters. "You think it'll be dark soon?"

"Dark? Not until our time together is up."

"What if I just stayed here?"

"What do you mean? Stay here forever?"

The ends of the braids bobbed up and down in reply.

"That's not an option, Little Self."

"Yeah, I figured. Do you think I'll have time to get home before it gets dark, though? I mean, when it's time for me to go?"

The old woman frowned and tilted her head down to peer into the Child's face. "What's all this sudden concern with the darkness? I've never known you to be afraid to be out alone in the woods after dark."

The little one piped up. "Oh. Oh, no! I'm not afraid of the woods after dark, that's not what I was getting at. I just wondered how soon darkness would fall after I went out the garden gate, that's all. I was just wondering how long the twilight would hold when our meeting was over. It could just suddenly be night or it could sorta fade to dark. Know what I mean?"

"You made it clear enough." Grandma seemed pensive. "I really can't answer your question, though. I suppose we'll just have to see what's what when it happens." She patted the small knee patch. "Eh? We're treading new ground here. We'll just have to wait and see what surprises await us."

The Child agreed. She again scanned the shadowed forest. Her gaze rose and panned the different ridgetops.

"What, Little Self? What's bothering you?"

"I think a lot of people are scared of the woods at night." She momentarily brought her hand to her chest for emphasis. "I'm not, you understand, but I think a lot of people are. When you brought that 'afraid' business up, it made me think of other scary things, things in the world that I do think are scary."

"Oh? Like what kind of things?"

Little Self pursed her lips. "Mostly how some people act," she said. "Their bad behavior. That's scary. But what I was specifically thinking about was how society lets a majority opinion or belief control their response or acceptance of reality."

"My, that was a mouthful. I suppose you have an example of this 'control' that's so scary to you?"

"Yep, I do."

The old woman waited to hear it.

The Child looked down at her scuffed shoes as they swung in and out, kicking the heels against the rough masonry wall.

Patiently, the Crone waited for Little Self's example.

Thump-thump went the heels.

A small particle of concrete bounced down onto the flagstone pathway.

Waiting.

Thump-thump.

A second and third piece of stone fell and rolled.

"Are you going to kick down the entire wall from under us before you decide you're going to answer?"

Little Self giggled. "Nooo."

"Well then?"

"I was busy," defended the youngster.

"Busy kicking down my wall."

"No, busy thinking."

"I see."

"Granny?"

"Yes?"

"Why do people let a majority opinion rule reality?"

"Wait a minute, Missy. You were supposed to give me an example, remember?"

"Oh yeah, I forgot," she grinned behind the hand that shot up to her mouth to cover her embarrassment. "My example was the millennium—the false one, I mean."

"Ahhh," the old woman crooned with a knowing nod, "now I get it. That example certainly pinpoints your concern a lot better."

"In my time, when the New Year's Eve of 1999 came, everyone acted like it was the true millennium just because they wanted the year 2000 to mark it instead of the real year of 2001. Even the TV had special programming on it and every news station ran historical recaps of the millennium. Everybody got into playing a part of the misconception. Everybody got into the act so the misconception got stronger and stronger." Exasperated, the Child threw up her arms. "Nobody stuck to the facts—the reality of it! It was awful. It was so scary to me watching how everybody caved into the popular opinion of 2000 being the millennium and then celebrating it." Eyes widened to full moons. "Granny! Some even thought it was the end of the world!"

"Yes, yes," soothed the old woman while again patting the knee, "I know. I know."

"Well?" Little Self impatiently pushed. "Don't you think that was scary? Wasn't it really scary to see even media people—the newspeople—cave in to a false premise of reality? Even when their minds knew the true date?"

"Yes, I do, Honey. I'd have to agree that whenever reality is altered through popular opinion, that that's a very scary thing, indeed. Intellectually, yes, people knew the true date of the actual millennium. Those such as the media folks recognized the actual reality, Little Self. Yet you have to understand that public pressure is a very powerful element in society and . . ."

"To the point of ignoring the facts?" the upset Child hastily interjected. "To the point of completely negating reality?"

A cautioning finger quickly came up. "Watch it, now. Ignoring, yes; negating, no. No one's personal opinion or belief can ever act to negate facts or reality—ever. Watch your words, Child, watch your words here. Don't let your excitement jumble the truth of it with unintended exaggerations."

Springing off the garden wall, the Child duly accepted her elder's admonition. She fretted before the seated one. "But why, Granny? I don't understand how something like that could happen?

"People have intelligence," she said, pacing before the Crone. "If they know the facts of a certain reality, how can they so quickly and easily be swept up in such an obvious falsehood? Or how can they just sit back and let those others' beliefs end up becoming the mass behavior of the majority?" The little one shook her head. "I don't get it. I just don't get it."

"Stop spinning your wheels trying to figure such quirky elements of human behavior. The fact of it is that the media had the power to counteract the public's majority opinion and keep to reality, but they didn't."

That knowledge didn't begin to satisfy the girl. She was looking for the bottom line reason. "Why didn't they?"

"I suppose you'd have to ask them, Little Self. Honey," she sighed, "we could spend days speculating on this or that reason, but in the end, you'd have to go ask the media folks to get a definitive answer right from the source."

"Mmm. Maybe it was too late by then," the Child postulated. "Do you think that the strength of the public's opinion had gotten too strong by then and that's why the media people didn't try to keep it straight?"

"Now you're doing that 'speculating' thing. Perhaps it was too late," she said, shrugging her shoulders, "perhaps not. The media folks have a certain responsibility to broadcast truth; at least the truth as can be known and proven as that which is incontrovertibly factual. They knew that the millennium didn't actually begin until the start of 2001.

"It was all so simple, really. Just as the number one hundred completes the time unit of a century, the year 2000 completes the unit of another counted millennium, making it an impossibility for the new one to begin before 2001. They, the scientists and media folks, knew that the year 2000 was the last and final year of the old millennium, they just failed to make it public soon enough and put proper emphasis on it for that 'majority' to intellectually process it."

"Well," said the Child in a tone of clear disappointment, "it sure was a stupid thing to do."

"Not do," the old woman corrected. "It was a stupid thing for the scientists and media people to not do."

"Whatever," came the return mumble.

"Whatever," Grandma sincerely echoed back.

Little Self looked up. "You don't seem as though you care much about what happened with all that millennium stuff."

"Oh, it's not that I don't care, Honey. It's more that it's done and done. It's history."

"But history is only made by people's behavior of today," she reasoned.

"While that's very true, you still can't change what's already happened."

"I know that, but people can still learn from what's happened—from history."

"Indeed they can."

"But they don't," came the dejected response.

"Not always, Little Self. Not always. Sometimes even when the truth is known, majority opinion and preferred beliefs still sway the day to cast a shadow over it."

The Crone further explained. "It's a choice, isn't it? Doesn't it all come down to each and every individual making their own choice whether or not to believe in the truth of something or a falsehood that the majority is perpetuating by their insistent behavior?"

Reluctantly, almost imperceptibly, the Child nodded.

Chapter Twenty

The two sat together on the stone wall.

The unspoken words between them were full of heart-felt emotion. They were those types of silences that conveyed so much more than words ever could.

A soft breeze hushed through the pine branches as the light wind floated along the heavily-forested ridge lines and passed as an unseen spectral traveler through the ethereal glow of twilight.

Long wispy strands of hair, reflecting like spun silver in the mystical light, lifted gracefully in response to the traveler's passing.

Stray threads of loose dark brown filament, touched with a hint of deep auburn, wafted like a fringed aura about the Child's head.

Together they looked like a pair of supernatural beings in a legendary garden of ancient folklore. Together they looked like a nature pixie visiting the Old Woman of the Woods—the wise and aged Mother Nature.

"Granny," the Child softly said, adding her sweet voice to that of the shushing Wind Spirit's, "may I ask another question? About a different subject?"

The motion of the old one's nodding response sent an

errant strand of hair escaping from her head. It caught an air current and gracefully wavered away like a silken thread of a spider's silvery web.

"That book about us, about this time we spent together, did people understand it? I mean, really?"

"On the whole, they did."

The Child pensively bit her lip. "I know that there's a lot of aspects to the concept to understand, but what I want to specifically know is if people realized that you and I aren't separate spirits dwelling in the Mother's consciousness. I think that would be an easy misconception to slip into and it's important to recognize the big difference."

"Oh, there were some who never got it right. They preferred to claim that the Mother was talking about the concept of multiple personalities."

"That's what I was afraid of," frowned the Child.

"It's anticipated, isn't it? That 'twisting of words' thing we talked about earlier? Little Self, that kind of behavior will always be evident in society. If the Mother writes that something is white, there will always be someone out there who will swear she's really saying that it's black. You can't get away from that type of thing because it seems to be such a strongly ingrained part of some folk's nature. Some people just naturally read additional material into what others say or write. They look for hidden messages. They attempt to lift up the words and peer beneath them in search for suspected secret meanings. It's just their nature, is all."

"Like a personality fault."

"Flaw," the elder corrected. "Flaw's the word you want. We'd be more precise if we called it what it really is. It's an intellectual flaw, a flaw in one's thought process. It involves their level of intellectual perception and whether or not they perceive with unbiased clarity or with personal opinions that alter that clarity—alter the solid reality of What Is. It's a way of fitting life into one's self-styled reality."

"Okay, so you're saying that most people understood that we're—you and I—are just different aspects of one person's consciousness."

"That's what I'm saying. Most understood the reality of the concept. They understood that you and I are not two separate spirits crowding the private space of a primary third."

Little Self was visibly relieved.

The perceptive Crone eyed the youngster seated beside her. "There's more behind your concern, isn't there?"

"It occurred to me that, if people thought we were separate spirits, they'd also think that we were automatons."

The Crone broke out in a sudden burst of laughter after hearing the Child's choice of wording. "Autonomous! That's the word you want."

"Yeah," Little Self grinned without showing a smidgen of embarrassment, "that's the word I meant. Anyway," she eagerly continued, "it'd be wrong for people to think our aspects are autonomous. We're not separate spirits who can incarnate. I mean, the three of us can't interchange roles in different lifetimes or anything like that."

"I'm not even sure what you're getting at, Little Self. Are you meaning that, in another life time, some people might think that you could be the primary consciousness aspect and I be the Child Within aspect?"

"Uh-huh. Like switching places in different incarnations."

"Oh, my goodness, that would be a serious misconception." Then the old woman sighed. "Do you ever take a breather from thinking?"

That brought a giggle. "I only want to understand things."

"Things!" Granny repeated. "You want to understand *every* thing." She softened, "Child, it goes far beyond that. More than wanting understanding, you want all these every things to be *right*."

"And that's too much to want, isn't it," came the perceptive statement.

"I think it is. Yes, Honey, I think it is."

Head down, small fingers idly fiddling with Raggedy Ann's apron, the Child asked, "Is it wrong then?"

"It's never wrong for people to want things in the world to be right. Yet sometimes certain wants are beyond reason. Sometimes they turn into expectations.

"Everyone's different, Little Self. Every single person walking on this beautiful planet thinks a bit differently than every other individual they pass on the street or in the mall. They have different ways of perceiving reality. They have separate opinions, personalized attitudes, and behavioral factors such as intolerance and prejudice that alter viewpoints from those of clarity to those being voluntarily colored—sometimes twisted like we talked about. That's the reality, Little Self. That's the societal reality that must be accepted. To expect anything else is unreasonable—just plain unreasonable. To do so is not being fair to yourself."

"Unfair," repeated the little girl.

"Why, yes, Child. To do so causes inner anguish over the behavior of others caused by their misperceived thought processes. Isn't that exactly what we're talking about here? Isn't that precisely what you're feeling?"

"Yes," came the whispered admission.

"Well then, why do that to yourself?

The small shoulders hunched up and slumped back down. "I dunno."

"Ohhh, I think you do."

The small face upturned. "I do?"

"Mmmm, I think you do.

"Well, in that case, I don't know what kind of answer I'm supposed to give then. All I know is that I want people to see reality for what it is. All I know is that I want things like solid concepts to be seen in their purity instead of being colored or twisted out of shape."

A gnarled hand reached out to lift the Child's dejected chin.

Two sets of richly-colored mahogany eyes met.

"And that's a very noble want to have, Little Self. But, sorry to say, it's a bit too noble. It's too noble and too unreasonable to reach for, because it doesn't factor in the reality of people's intellectual and psychological differences."

"But the Mother has worked so hard to make all her concepts so simple, words so clear."

Silence.

The Wind Spirit whispered, "Shhhhh."

"Well, hasn't she worked hard doing that?"

Silence.

The Child hopped off the wall and stood her ground before the elder. "Huh?"

The old woman's voice was barely audible. "You're taking this personally, Little Self."

"No, I'm not."

"Much, much too personally, Honey."

The Child vehemently shook her head, braids swinging about in obstinate emphasis.

"Yes, you are because everyone's working hard."

A hard vee formed the unspoken question between the fine hair of the delicate dark brows.

"Yes, everyone," repeated the Crone. "The priest works hard to keep his flock gathered tightly together. The rabbi also. The Republican, the Democrat, the Independent, and all those in between work hard to keep their individual ideologies true to form. The atheist works hard to continue denying the concept of deities. The skeptic works hard to try to undermine certain realities. The born-agains work hard to convert all they meet.

"On and on, Little Self. On and on everyone is working hard to perpetuate his or her specialized beliefs and convictions. That's how you're taking this personally. You're on the Mother's side—deeply ensconced in her camp—and you're causing yourself inner anguish when others choose to remain on the outside or around the perimeter. But you can't do that. You must recognize the existence of the hundreds of thousands of other camps."

No response came.

"You're too close. You're not only in the Mother's camp, you're in her mind—her consciousness."

"So doesn't that alone explain why I'm taking this so personally?"

"You admit it, then? You admit that you're doing that?"

The Child nodded.

"That's a good start to understanding all this, then."

"So?" the girl prompted. "So where does that take us?"

"So it takes us right back to recognizing the purpose of the Mother's work. It takes us right back to the basic reason for her even being here."

"To give certain messages."

"To re-give them, Little Self. To breath freshness into timeless concepts, to wash away the dust of misconceptions that has settled on them over time. She has not come to convert."

Silence.

"She has not come to convert," the old woman was sure to restate. "Only to refresh age-old truths, only to place them once again before the masses. It's not her purpose to force anyone to partake."

The elder heard a deep sigh escape from the Child as she turned to slowly trace a circle pattern of pacing around the flagstones. The worn rubber soles of her shoes made no sound except when a footfall found a fallen lilac or aspen leaf.

"Okay then," the Child reasoned, beginning to puzzle through, "I'm an aspect of the Mother's consciousness and I'm not supposed to feel anxiety over how people twist her words? I'm not supposed to get upset over things like that?"

"That's right, Little Self, you're not."

Circling. Thinking.

Waiting.

"And I'm not supposed to feel deflated when people spread stupid rumors like falsely saying that she's implying that she's some goddess?"

Silvery, wispy hairs wafted in the light breeze. "No, you're not supposed to feel deflated over that, nor angry, nor hurt."

The pacing quickened.

Waiting.

"But it's the Mother these people are lying about," she tried defending.

"All the more reason," came the unexpected reply.

"All the more reason? What? All the more reason to not have those feelings?"

"Yes, Little Self, all the more reason."

"You're not making any sense to me," admitted the Child with complete honesty. "That just doesn't make a bit of sense."

"Is that what you think?"

"Yes."

"Truly?"

"Yes, Granny. Truly."

"Then you're missing something, something very, very important here."

The Child's face scrunched up. She held Raggedy Ann tighter to her chest, yet said nothing.

Neither did the old woman who wisely waited out the young one's thought process.

Pacing.

The Crone gazed up into the shadowy timberline.

The pacing movement halted in midstep as the Child turned to lock eyes with the elder's.

Sensing an epiphany had sprung forth within the other's mind, the old woman raised a questioning brow.

"She's not why she's here," Little Self said. "What people say about her isn't important to the purpose."

Though the Crone wanted to smile wide with the Child's realization, she didn't. "That's right, she's not here for her. Little Self, come here," she softly requested, reaching out her hand for the Child's.

The little girl slowly closed the distance between them and stood before the elder's knees.

Weathered hands smoothed over the sides of the denim coveralls. "How many times has the Mother put in writing the idea—the reality—that she's no different from everyone else? How many times has she strived to downplay her own personality, her own identity and beingness?"

The Child's gaze slid down to the doll. "Lots," she reticently mumbled.

"Uh-huh. And how many times has she said that she's here just to write of certain messages? That she's nothing higher or greater or better than anyone else?"

"Lots."

"Little Self, the Mother is not the Word either. She is not even the Voice of the Word. If anything, if you had to classify her as anything, you might liken her to being some type of amplifier for the Voice of the Word." The Crone smiled. "Maybe like a bullhorn. Do you understand what that means?"

The Child looked back up. "I'm not a baby," she reminded. "It means that she's just emphasizing. Her purpose is to re-emphasize the messages that people forgot."

"That's right, Honey. So if she's not here for her, why get upset over what others say about her?

Little Self self-consciously shrugged.

"Isn't getting the messages down in black and white again what's ultimately the most important aspect of her purpose?"

"Yessss."

"Well? Well then?"

"Well then, am I not supposed to have feelings? I love the Mother. It hurts when people say bad and mean things about her."

"Oh, Honey," cooed the Crone while reaching for the Child's hand. "Of course, you're supposed to have feelings. Why, it's your wonderful childlike nature that gives the Mother such a wild freedom to outwardly express her own happiness and spontaneous joy so many times. It's your childlike freedom and innocence that gives her those wildly uninhibited and heartfelt reactions to nature! Like when she runs out dancing in a moonlit snowfall." Granny smiled. "Barefoot no less. It's you who does that. You!"

Little Self suppressed a grin of embarrassment.

"Oh, Dear Heart, don't you see? Your sensitive feelings have saved the Mother from excessive grief many times. Your feelings that bleed through to her come as counted blessings in her life, blessings she always recognizes as such. You, Little Self, you do that. You do that with your feelings!"

The Child's fingers twisted the doll's dress fabric.

"Then why am I not allowed to have bad feelings too?"

"Because the ones you're talking about are brought on by personalizing the Mother's work and the misperceptions others have of her as an individual. You're causing yourself far too much grief by placing equal emphasis on the Mother and the work. It's the work, Little Self. It's the work that takes priority. It doesn't matter at all, not one iota, what's said about the Mother. And if you let those things upset you, then it's because you're forgetting the proper arrangement of her own priorities."

"But it's not nice to say bad things about people."

"Did I say it was? Did I once say or imply that?"

"No, but those things still hurt."

"Not if you don't let them, Little Self. Not if you see yourself and the Mother as merely secondary elements behind the primary purpose. She's like the bookbinder who works behind the scenes, putting text pages of words together. It's the texts that are the primary issue, isn't it? That bookbinder just makes some of them happen."

The Child thought about that and nodded. Her nod was not the final word, though. "It's still not nice to say bad things about people."

"No, Little Self," the old woman smiled with tender sensitivity, "there's no denying that. Saying bad things about people certainly isn't a nice thing for anyone to do."

"Somebody ought to tell them, then," the Child grumbled back.

Without responding, the elder's heart smiled with the knowing that somebody had just done that very thing . . . a very special little somebody.

Chapter Twenty-One

Granny leaned to the Child's ear and whispered secretively, "Don't look now, but we've got a curious visitor."

Eyes suddenly widening, the little girl whispered in reply, "Where?"

"Move very slowly," the Crone advised, "so as not to startle her off. Behind you, just beyond the fence."

In slow motion the Child rotated her head to peek at the secret visitor. Spying it, her heart raced as her anxiety suddenly spiked through the roof. "Oh!" she softly exclaimed, "Hurry! Hurry, Granny! Go get the gun and scare it away!"

The cream-colored coyote cocked its head.

"Little Self," the old woman quietly reminded, "we don't need to do that anymore. We don't have little dogs to protect. Now we let the coyotes roam wherever they wish."

"Oh yeah, I forgot," came the sheepish reply. "You don't have dogs anymore. In my time . . ."

"Yes, I know. In your time the Mother and Sally scare off the predator types like the bears, cougars, and coyotes with loud noises."

Surreptitiously, the Child peeked again at the coyote. Slowly she turned to face it. "Hi, Ms. Coyote," she gently greeted before giving it a bit of sound advice and what she considered fair warning. "You'd better start getting in the habit of visiting somewhere else 'cause Granny's gonna be getting a puppy soon."

Grandma rapidly tapped the little one's arm and whispered, "Will you quit with that?"

Keeping her eyes on the coyote, the Child responded. "You said you'd think about it. You said you promised."

"Yes, I said I'd promise to think about it. And I certainly intend to keep that promise, but in the meantime, don't you think you're jumping to conclusions? Don't you think you're jumping straight into a deep pile of expectation?"

With solid assurance, Little Self piped back with a mischievous grin, "Nope!"

"Ohhh, I see. You think you know my mind, do you?"

Turning back around to face the Crone, Little Self cleverly asked, "Aren't we of the same mind? Kinda?"

Without explanation, the old woman began closely examining the Child's coveralls. She bent forward and squinted as her eyes roved over the bib, along the sides, and down the leg seams. "Turn around," she requested with firm pressure applied to the waist to urge the little body around.

"What're you doing?" Little Self asked, turning.

"Mmmm, just looking."

"Looking for what?"

"A tag. The brandname tag."

"It's right here," the Child said, tugging on the label. "Why do you need to see the brandname tag?"

"To see what it says, why else?"

"It says OshKosh."

"Nope. Wrong tag. There's got to be another," declared the Crone while searching about the overalls.

"Why do you think there's another one?"

"Has to be."

"Why?

"Because I think it says 'Made by SmartyPants!'"

Giggling over that, the Child whipped back around to face the elder. "That was funny," she laughed as though being tickled.

"Shhh," warned the old woman, quickly covering the girl's lips with a crooked finger. "Don't make any sudden moves like that or you'll scare our guest away."

Little Self peered back at the coyote.

It had sidled up closer to the fence and was sitting up to attention as though waiting for tea time to begin and expecting to be served. It seemed that being scared was the last emotion from its mind.

"You think it looks hungry, Granny? You think we look tasty?"

"Oh, for heaven's sake. Now look who's being silly. A little Yorkie pup, yes, but certainly not a human. You know that as well as I do."

"Still . . ."

"Want to go back inside?"

Again the Child snuck a furtive peek at the animal that didn't look as though it was ready to leave any time soon. "I'm not scared," she proudly declared.

A silvery brow arched. "Did I say you were?"

"Well . . . maybe we could go back in."

The old woman eyed the little one. "You sure you're not scared? Just a teeny bit?"

"Nope. Maybe if we went back inside the coyote will go away, so the raccoons can come back on the porch again. I don't think they were done eating."

"Ohhh, I see," the Crone cooed. "Well, maybe you're right about that. Let's do that and see what happens, shall we?"

Seeing how slowly the old woman rose from the stone wall and took the time to bend backwards to stretch her back, the Child grabbed a gnarled hand and gently tugged. "C'mon," she prompted with urgency, pulling toward the steps, "the raccoon family is probably waiting for that coyote to leave."

"You think?"

"Yes! C'mon!"

Halfway up the rustic railroad tie steps, Grandma was feeling playful. She purposely stopped to point down at the garden. "Look how well those foxgloves did this year. My goodness, they grew strong and tall. And see? Over there, those . . ."

"Granny! The raccoons! You're forgetting about the coons!"

Returning her attention to the issue at hand, the old one acted like she hadn't remembered. "Oh, yes, that's right. The raccoons. Okay, let's get ourselves back into the house then."

Hand in hand they gained entry.

A sigh managed to audibly slip from the Child's lips. "There, that's better."

"For whom, I wonder?" Grandma suspiciously inquired.

Little Self didn't seem to hear, at least that's how she chose to react to the semi-sarcastic comment.

"Want something to eat?" the elder asked while ignoring the slick way the Child avoided the former question. "Are you hungry?"

"No, I'm fine."

"Not even a snack?"

The braids moved back and forth when the Child shook her head in reply.

"Okay then, what would you like to do?"

"I don't need entertaining. What I mean is that we don't have to be doing anything special on my account. Just being here with you is enough doing for me."

"You took the words right out of my mouth, Child. Still, it might be nice to busy ourselves at something together." She winked. "Might keep our minds off the time."

"Whatever you want, Granny. How much time do you think we have left?"

"I don't imagine too much more. You've been here for quite a while already."

"How will we know? Do you think we'll know when it's time or do you think . . . ?"

The Child's question was halted by a sudden howl of the coyote that pierced the crystal clear twilight air.

Grandma spookily widened her eyes.

Little Self laughed and teasingly hit at the old one's arm. "That wasn't scary," she declared with false conviction.

"Who said anything about scary?"

Seeing that the conversation was heading nowhere, the Child ended it with a single word: "Nobody."

"That's what I thought," the Crone underscored while turning to reach into a pantry cupboard and rummage through it.

"I'm not hungry," the Child reminded.

Instead of sounding like a nagging old hag by telling the youngster that she'd just made a false assumption, the old woman simply said, "I remember. These old ears may look old and decrepit on the outside but the insides still hear every little sound." She then began humming while pulling items from the shelves and handing them off into the small receiving hands.

When Little Self finally had to use her chin to balance the tip of the towering armful, she mumbled through clenched teeth, "Am I supposed to put all this stuff somewhere?"

Turning with skirts billowing out and fingers fluttering before the girl's eyes, the Crone exclaimed, "Well go, Child, go put all those things on the kitchen table!"

Carefully balancing her load, Little Self shuffled off to the table and gently removed one item at a time. Four large coffee cans full of halved eggshells, a mortar and pestle, a small cardboard box of what looked like bones, and several well-used pie plate tins. The Child thought it all very curious and couldn't imagine what all these things were used for. Peeking into the box of bones, she anxiously inquired, "What're we going to do with all this stuff?"

"Eggshells 'n' bones," the Crone chanted. "Eggshells 'n' bones." That was all she said as she arranged all the items in their proper order for working with. Then she sat.

Little Self stood at the opposite side of the table waiting for instructions.

Surveying the table, a frown deepened the crevice between the silver brows. "Oh, my, we forgot the rolling pin and cutting board. Would you be a dear and go get those for us?"

Eager to be of help, the Child raced to the right drawers and returned in a flash. She held them high aloft. "Ta-da! One rolling pin, one cutting board," she announced with a broad, pixie-like smile.

"Good. You keep those. Those are your tools."

"Okay. What do I do with these tools of mine?"

"You spread those baked bones out on the cutting board and crush them with the rolling pin."

"Uh-huh. And . . . why do I do this?"

"For next year's garden, of course."

"Of course," Little Self repeated without understanding, "how silly of me." Then she beamed as the light bulb came on. "Bonemeal!"

"Yes! And once these eggshells are crushed down like fine powder with the mortar and pestle, we add the two together and make a wonderful garden nutrient compound—all completely natural. In the springtime and throughout the summer months we work this in the soil several times along with that good peat we get from down below in the valley."

"No wonder your flowers are doing so well. Okay," the Child said, delicately placing two bones from the box onto the cutting board, "do I just start rolling these?"

"Humph. Going to take you forever if you're planning on only doing two at a time," Granny said, pulling out six more bones and clanking them down on the board. "There, now you're in business."

Holding the rolling pin in mid-air, Little Self hesitated before bringing it down. "I just start rolling away?"

"No, not exactly. The rolling part's easier if you first get them cracked down into manageable pieces. So first you want to use the pin to put pressure on them to break them up a bit. Baking the bones twice in the oven makes it easy. Go ahead, Dear, just start leaning down on the pin and those old bones'll start falling apart."

The Child made a furtive attempt and smiled after seeing how easy it was. "This isn't so hard."

"Would I give you the hard part?"

Hearing that, the Child was concerned. "Is the eggshell part harder? If it is I'll be glad to do that instead," she said, raising her hands for the elder's inspection. "I have strong hands for my age."

The Crone made an exaggerated face of amazement. "You must get those strong hands from climbing all those trees and fences."

"Yep."

"No, Child, neither part is hard. All I do with these halved eggshells is like so." She demonstrated. "First I fill the pie tin with shells and place the paper plate over them like this. Then I take my hand and apply pressure to crush them down, just like you first did with the bones. Now," she said while pouring the broken pieces into the mortar, "now I grind them down to salt-sized particles." She lowered the half-filled mortar to her lap for better leverage.

"The grinding's the hardest part of this operation. After awhile it can get to the middle of your palm and, if you're not careful, you can end up with a blister there. I just work at it at an easy pace. No need to do them all at once. Little projects like this keep me busy—always something to do around here—no bored old ladies live in this woodland cottage."

That made the Child grin, for she knew better than any other that this granny, no matter how old she looked to others, would never ever be bored.

Chapter Twenty-Two

While both the Child and the Crone were keeping their hands busy with repetitive motions, their minds were free to explore whatever thoughts came to them.

For a time, the Grandmother talked of some of the humorous experiences she'd had while out in the deep woods gathering kindling, puffballs, and other types of fungi. She was a wellspring of amusing tales full of visually descriptive details and anecdotes—some of which were hilarious, others philosophical. She appeared to be one of those storytellers one never tired of listening to.

When an extended pause of silence came between tales, Little Self took advantage of it to interject yet another question. "Granny?"

"Mmmm? Tired of my yakking, are you?"

"Oh, no," the Child was quick to dispel, "not at all. Never. I just happened to think of something to ask you, that's all."

"You sure?"

"Of course, I'm sure."

"Because if you're not, just tell this old woman to quit spinning her yarns. Won't hurt my feelings one bit."

"No way! I love hearing all those tales. I like the funny

ones, but I especially like the others that show how the Old Woman of the Woods—the elder Mother Nature—has so many lessons to teach people through nature's behavior. Oh, no, Granny, I'm really, really not tired of your stories. I'm really, really not."

"Okay, you don't have to go overboard here, you've convinced me. Go ahead then, shoot with your question."

Little Self stood at the table, the small body rhythmically bending back and forth at the waist while working to roll out the broken bones. The meter didn't change pace as the question was voiced. "It seems to me that there are times that whenever there's a choice to be made; doing the most spiritual thing—choosing the most spiritual option—isn't always the best."

Silence.

Crushing sounds filled the air.

Grandma spoke softly. "Every decision has options attached or there'd be no decision at all to make. Likewise, every single one of those options carries its own slew of varying elements; some spiritual, some not. And it sounds to me like you've concluded that, sometimes, the most spiritual option is not always the best course of action to take. Do I understand what you're saying? Am I right?"

"Yes. Right. Whaddya think?"

"Though your premise, on the surface, sounds a bit contrary to following a path of spiritual behavior, it's not. I would concur with your thinking on that, Little Self. I would indeed concur."

Small eyes glimmered. "You would?"

The Crone joked. "And just what don't you understand about the term 'concur'?"

The Child giggled. "Nothing. I mean . . ."

"Uh-huh," Grandma hummed while rotating the pestle around and around. "So what got you thinking about this somewhat unusual premise of yours?"

"Oh, just different situations I've observed throughout the Mother's time, I guess. She always says that 'whenever a decision has to be made, one should always make the determining factor be based on which option is the most spiritual one to do.'"

"And you don't agree with that?"

"Well . . . " she hesitated. "I do and I don't."

"Are you sitting on the fence then?"

"Ummm," she considered. "No, not on the fence, exactly. Maybe jumping over it; you know, going back and forth."

"Back and forth? Oh, well then, wouldn't that mean that you can't decide? Seems to me that that'd be like saying something's both black and white at the same time."

Beneath Little Self's hands, the motion of the rolling pin stopped.

The Child pulled herself to her full height and immediately scrunched up her face. "Then that's definitely not what I mean because something can't be both ways, can't be both black and white."

"That's true, however . . ."

"There's a 'but' in there somewhere's, isn't there."

"You could say that."

"I knew it," the Child said. "I knew there was something I was missing—had to be because it bothered me that I couldn't agree one hundred percent with the Mother's saying."

The Crone placed a fresh round of eggshell halves in the tin pan and set the paper plate over it. She pressed the center down and worked her fingers out toward the edges, crushing them in preparation for the mortar stage. "I think we could sort all of this out better if we had some type of example to pick apart. Did you have one in mind, Dear?"

Returning to her bone rolling, Little Self admitted that she had. "Uh-huh. When Sally was in Kansas City and called the Mother to ask her opinion about bringing Sally's mother, Mary Belle, back to Colorado to live with them, the Mother said doing so would be the spiritual thing to do. So that's what they did. That's why they did it."

"Yes, go on, Child."

"Well . . ."

"And you have second thoughts on that decision—the reason for it?"

"Well," the girl hedged, "Sally's mother had Alzheimer's and things got really bad. Her behavior got so . . . umm, so . . ."

"Unpredictable?" tried the Crone.

"Yeah, unpredictable because one hour she'd be sweet and almost normal and the next hour she'd be screaming out the window and biting people. It was really stressful because it was so crazy-like around there for a few years. I don't think everyone could've handled that much stress, because not everyone's cut out for handling that kind of daily situation. Not everyone comes equipped with that kind of constitution, so then that 'spiritual' decision becomes a personally deterrent one."

"Detrimental," the old woman kindly corrected with a smile. "It becomes a personally *detrimental* one."

"De-tri-men-tal," the Child slowly repeated. "Yeah. Sooo, the way I see it," she continued, "if a decision, whether it's the spiritual one or not, ends up harming the decision-maker in some way or turns into a huge detrimental situation, it isn't really the right one to make. I mean, in the long run." Little Self frowned and scratched her head. "I'm not sure I said all that right."

"Sure you did. You did just fine. Do you think the Mother and Sally shouldn't have made that decision?"

"Oh, no! I don't mean them. This isn't about them. I mean, not really. It's just that I saw how hard the caregiving became when Mary Belle got worse and how easily certain behaviors caused the caregivers added work and stress. That's what I'm talking about. I just can't believe that every single person on this planet could get through the same type of thing without being somehow seriously affected." Little Self sighed then. "With Alzheimer's or brain diseases like it . . . well, it's just not a situation that everybody can take on, especially not as an at-home caregiver where there's little or no time to get away to spend time with normal people."

"Ahhh, I see," nodded the Crone. "So you're thinking that this specific philosophical statement that the Mother made is too much of a *blanket* statement. Is that it?"

"Yes! That's it!" the excited Child impishly piped. "That's exactly it! I don't think it should be a blanket statement, because there are just some situations that shouldn't be shoved into it. It took both of them together to care for Mary Belle, so they had each other to com . . . com . . . " The Child impatiently shook her hands in frustration with herself for not being able to come up with the word she knew she wanted.

"Commiserate," Granny quickly filled in.

"Yeah, to commiserate with."

The elder's brow rose. "That's a pretty big word for a six-year-old."

The rolling pin stopped in mid-roll when Little Self stood tall, taking a stately stance with dramatized airs. Simulating the pose of a pampered prima ballerina, her little angular arms tried to effect gracefulness as they slowly lifted out at her sides. "See me?" she exclaimed while attempting to make a smooth twirl like a runway model, "I just *look* six-years old! I may look like a little girl on the outside, but inside—in our shared consciousness—I hear the Mother use lots and lots of big words! Tons of 'em."

Grinning at seeing the outlandish theatrics, Granny agreed. "I suppose you do at that, Child. Can't be helped."

Immediately dropping the charade once her point was made and returning to the work at hand, Little Self continued her thoughts. "Anyway, as I was saying," she emphasized, "Sally and the Mother were lucky because they had each other to share the workload and stress. They had each other to talk things over with. What about the caregivers who have to do it all alone? Or people who have small children at home? Or others who have to work full-time jobs? Or . . . well, I think there's all kinds of other reasons why caring for a parent at home who has Alzheimer's would not be the best choice . . . even if it is the most spiritual one to choose."

Silence.

"Don't you, Granny?"

"Stile."

Little Self crinkled her face. "What?"

"Stile," came the single echo.

"Are we still talking about the same thing? Diddya just change the subject?"

The Crone smiled. "Yes, we most certainly are still talking about the same thing and no, I did not change the subject. Stile, Little Self, that's the word you want to properly describe where you're at with this. That fence. Remember? You were talking about that 'fence' you didn't think you were sitting on."

"Ohhh, a stile! Now I get it, she piped up with a grin. "You mean one of those old-fashioned wooden steps country people build to go up and down over the top of a fence instead of putting in a gate. Yeah, I get it!"

"Mmmm, thought you would. A stile quite naturally represents those extenuating circumstances that can be applied to every situation—every concept, too. You don't need to sit on a fence with a concept or an issue nor make yourself dizzy going back and forth from one side to the other. The stile lets you use extended reason and logic to factor in those extenuating circumstances with complete acceptability.

"You see, Child, when making tough decisions, the spirituality of each choice must indeed be a priority. I'm not saying it shouldn't. However, every possible element of each different choice must also be considered and weighed. By this I mean . . . well, let's take your example.

"When it was decided to take Mary Belle into the home because 'it was the spiritual thing to do,' neither Sally nor the Mother factored in their own selves. Their decision was solely based on what the spiritual thing to do for one's mother was. When situations involve several people, you must not forget to give consideration to how that decision will affect all parties involved or else the decision is based on a single factor instead of all of them."

"I see what you mean about the extenuating circumstances, but in all fairness, they didn't know Mary Belle had Alzheimer's when they took her in."

"Yes, that is true, yet my point remains the same. All people involved must be factored into any decision. When this is done, those extenuating circumstances may begin to show their faces and greatly alter the total picture."

Silence.

Grandma peered over at the Child. "Is something wrong?"

"No, I only want to say that they were never sorry about their decision. My original point in bringing the whole thing up was the problem I was having with that saying of the Mother's."

"You think perhaps people don't already know that

there are extenuating circumstances to everything . . . even to philosophical sayings?"

"Maybe that's what I'm trying to get at. I just know how a lot of people take everything she says as black and white, that's all. I think the Mother maybe shouldn't have said 'always' in that saying because it didn't leave any room for those 'circumstances' that can change so much."

The old woman pursed her lips and rested back in her chair to think about what the Child had said. After a time, she commented on it. "Her words are carefully chosen, Little Self."

"Yes, I know that. And that's why I think she should've replaced the 'always' word with a different one. Maybe 'usually' or 'most often' would've fit better. I don't know," she shrugged, "all I know is that there was something about that saying that always bothered me a little bit and now I know what it was."

"So you think it should be fixed somehow?"

Little Self nodded.

Knowing a secret element about their meeting that the Child was not yet apprised, the old woman said, "Maybe you just did."

"Did what?"

"Why, fix it, Honey. Fix it."

"You're not making any sense to me. I can't fix anything the Mother says. I'm only an aspect of her consciousness."

"That you are, Child. Indeed, that you are," she readily agreed while leaning over the table toward the little one. She whispered as though giving a hidden clue to uncovering the meaning of her statement. "Yet never underestimate probabilities . . . especially," she cryptically hushed, "especially those wonderful *possibilities*."

"Possibilities," the Child softly repeated beneath her breath. "Poss-i-bil-i-ties."

Chapter Twenty-Three

The girl respectfully held the word on her tongue, savoring it like a mystical morsel of magic. She rose from the chair and went to stand at the glass door of the deck. Silently inching the slider back, she slipped out and tiptoed across the worn planks to the rail. Holding her breath, she peered down.

"Coyote's gone," came the clear voice from behind.

The Child jumped at the sudden, unexpected sound and spun to see Grandma standing directly behind her. "You scared me!" she scolded.

"I did? I'm sorry about that. Why were you so jumpy?"

"I wasn't jumpy."

"Okay, if you say so," the Crone shrugged as she sidled up beside the youngster and cast her gaze down to where the coyote had previous sat watching them. "She's long gone. Guess there was nothing interesting to spark her curiosity once we came inside."

Little Self's eyes intently panned the underbrush below then scanned the valley beyond. "Where do you think she went?"

Knowing the Child was really asking if the grandma thought the coyote was still around, the Crone responded with confidence. "Oh, I think she's far away by now. You know how much ground those beauties can cover in a short time. I suspect she's long gone. Yes, she's long gone from here by now."

"You think?"

The breeze quickened at that moment as the Wind Spirit's deft fingers tenderly caressed the Crone's quicksilver tendrils. They gracefully lifted about her head like shafts of spun glass.

The Child noticed and the sight inspired a curious comment. "You have angel hair! You know, that stuff people use at Christmastime!"

Embarrassed, the old woman's cheeks flushed. Hands quickly raising to smooth down the mass of drifting strands, her flustering was interrupted when Little Self immediately reached for her hands to stop her.

"No!" she cried. "Don't touch it! You look magical like that!"

The color of the flushing cheeks deepened into a full-blown blush. "Ohhh, go on, don't be so silly. Why I'm just an old woman with wild, unruly hair." She harumphed. "Nothing magical about me at all."

The Child's grip on the elder's hands tightened. "Oh, yes, yes there is, Granny," she strongly affirmed while gazing up in mesmerized wonder at the floating strands. "You're very magical to me."

Before the Crone's eyes could be given the chance to mist, she forced them back with a laugh. "You say the strangest things, Little Self. My goodness, you certainly come up with some good ones."

Releasing her grip, the Child responded, "They're good ones because they're true."

As if on cue, each turned and began walking together along the deck's perimeter.

No sound passed between them save the squeak of a loose board or two.

No nighthawk called from the shadowy woods.

No owl hooted from nearby pines.

Coyote howls were stilled.

Then, the high firs began swaying and hushing with the approach of the Wind Spirit again. He was circling back for a better look at the two standing in the unusual, almost magical, twilight.

Granny's hair began to lift once more. She made an involuntary move to smooth it down then thought better of it; instead, she smiled down at the Child at her side. "Breeze is kicking up its heels again. It'll get a bit chilly out here. Let's get ourselves back inside."

The two headed for the sliding door and, after passing through, the Child made sure it was closed tight behind them.

They returned to their respective places at the table; the Grandmother tending to her work with the eggshells, the Child placing more twice-baked bones on the cutting board. Two pairs of hands; one small and smooth, the other bent and aged, attended to finishing up the projects they'd begun.

Little Self was first to speak again. "Granny?"

"Yes, Dear?"

"You did look magical out there, at least to me you did. And that made me think of magic. You know, the magical things in life."

"Magical? You want to talk about the magical things in life now?"

The Child nodded. "Uh-huh, if that's okay."

"Mmmm, the magical things in life," the old woman softly repeated.

Little Self found an opening to lightheartedly tease.

Playing the game to the hilt, she added a dramatic effect by shooting her little fists to her hips. "Granny," she sighed, "what exactly don't you understand about the word 'magical'?"

The Crone's brows arched in surprise. "Well! Aren't you the little opportunist." She leaned over the table, eyed the youngster, and flashed a wide grin. "Got me."

Little Self, completely satisfied with herself, giggled. "I was kinda afraid to do that."

"And, pray tell, why was that?"

"I was afraid you'd think it was disrespectful for a child to talk like that to an elder."

The Crone's eyes narrowed to slits. "Yet you did it anyway, eh?"

"Yeah, because I figured you'd be different."

"And was I?"

Proudly, the Child declared without question, "Yep!"

"Mmm, I see."

"Well, aren't you?"

"Oh, I don't know. What I do know is that everyone needs to feel free to express themselves, to feel free to be spontaneous. You certainly are that, Little Self," the old woman chided with a grin. "You certainly are that."

"So we can talk about magic then?"

"Remember earlier, when we clarified that we could talk about anything we wanted?"

Twin braids bobbed up and down with the nod.

"Are you absolutely sure about that? Are you positive you remember?"

"Sure I do."

The elder kept a straight face. "Then what exactly didn't you understand about the word 'anything'?"

The Child's mouth dropped open before tossing a bone fragment at her companion. She broke out in laughter. "You got me back!"

"Fancy that," came the smirking reply. "I wonder how that happened?" Then the Crone's eyes rounded in feigned spookiness. "Must've been magical."

"Nooo, nuh-uh," chanted the Child in a tone of disbelief. "That's silly. That's not magic."

In the blink of an owl's eye the mood of the room changed from playful to seriousness. "What is magic, Little Self?"

"Magic is . . . Things are magical when they . . ."

The Crone held back filling in the spaces the Child was leaving between her words. She patiently waited and listened for the full answer to come forth.

"Isn't magic when . . . ?"

"Now you're asking me. I asked you first. You tell me what magic is."

Little Self slouched back in her chair and intently stared into the eyes of the old woman as she tried to sort out her thoughts.

Grandma returned to her work while she waited.

And waited.

And waited some more.

While the old one's hands flew with tending to her work, her mind was following the Child's thought process and watching how the youngster's body language reflected the intense mental activity.

Little Self began fidgeting.

She sighed to herself.

In frustration, she pursed her lips and shook her head. Finally she spoke in a voice heavy with irritation. "Every time I think I have an example of magic it ends up being something else."

"Something else?"

"Yes," the Child seemed to pout. "It ends up being something that can be explained, something natural."

"Oh."

"Oh?"

"What I meant was, maybe you need more time to think of true examples then."

Little Self's eyes squinted at the Crone in skepticism. "There aren't any true examples of magic are there, Granny."

"Is that what you've concluded?"

"Is that your answer to my question?"

"It wasn't an answer, it was a question of my own. It sounded to me as though you think you've concluded that there are no definitive examples of true magic and I merely wanted to clarify whether or not that was what you were saying. Was it?"

In an effort to be absolutely sure of her answer, the Child hesitated several moments before responding. She mentally checked and double-checked her thinking. "Yes," she finally announced with surety, "my answer is yes, that's what I'm saying."

The old woman didn't make an immediate reply.

The Child waited. Squirming in her chair, she waited.

"Myth," the Crone eventually whispered, "is all true magic just myth? Could it be that it's all just so much myth? Is it only so much sparkling, glittering fairy dust of age-old myths and children's storybooks? Of ancient legends and fairy tales? Of the cottony fluff of an old storyteller's wildly creative imagination? If so, does such a thing as true magic even exist then?"

"You asked two questions," said the Child. "You asked a second question based on the answer to the first one."

"Indeed I did."

Little Self found that she was suddenly handed a basketful of entirely new ideas to sort out. Mentally, she set the woven container in her lap and began to, one by one, pick out the contents. She thoroughly analyzed each one, looking at it from every possible angle before setting it aside and giving her attention to the next one in the basket of collected conceptual elements.

After a time, she raised her eyes to the old woman's.

Grandma was busy with her pestle. "Finished?" she asked without having to look up.

"There's no such thing as true magic," proclaimed Little Self.

"Really."

"Yes, really."

"You sure about that?"

"Yes."

"Absolutely, positively sure about that?"

Though the Child was tempted to ask Granny what she didn't understand about the word "yes," she didn't. "Yes," was the singular reply.

None followed in return.

Now it was the Child's turn to wait.

The old woman exhaled a deep and long sigh as she finished grinding the shells in the mortar. Carefully emptying the powdered substance into the large coffee can, she sat back and looked at the Child who was eager for a response. Instead of giving one straight away, the elder arched her back and rubbed at it. "Sometimes this job ends up being harder than it looks," she mumbled. "Grinding for any length of time takes muscle that I don't seem to have anymore. Tsk-Tsk," she regrettably clucked, "getting old has some drawbacks I'd just as soon wish I could ignore."

The Child waited.

"But since I can't ignore them maybe I could just wave my magic wand over them and make them vanish, eh?"

The Child was locked in her own serious space and didn't think the comment particularly funny. She waited.

"Humph, guess that one was a dud," grumbled the Crone. "My audience seems to be a tough crowd to work tonight."

Little Self remained nonplused. She continued to wear her poker face like a painted-on mask.

Grandma folded her forearms on the table and bent forward. Resting her chin on them, she peered up at the small girl across from her. Softly, she said, "That ol' stoneface doesn't suit you, Little Self. It's far too serious for that pretty little face of yours."

One corner of the Child's mouth tipped up and cracked the stone.

"Well, that's a bit better," Grandma said with a widening smile. "Do you think we could push that smile a little further up those rosy cheeks?"

Little Self, determined to hold it right where it was, fought to keep the smile from sprouting and failed. It blossomed, petals spreading up both sides of her face.

"All right, then!" exclaimed the Crone as she sat back and slapped the tabletop. "Let's get this conversation back on the road!"

Ready to make some progress, the Child straightened herself in the chair.

"Little Self," the elder began, "magic is relative. The word 'magic' is relative to the conceptual terminology that society has attached to it. Know what I'm saying? We need to be clear on things as we drive down every mile of this road."

Nodding, the Child said she understood.

"Okay then," the Crone continued. "Society is confused on this. It's greatly confused. Are we agreed on that statement?"

Another nod came.

"So magic is off to a bad beginning right from the starting gate."

Little Self was already getting into this. She loved philosophical discussions. Now it was her turn to rest her chin on her arms. "Society has given the wrong name for magic's starting gate," she said. "Society calls the starting gate 'supernatural,' when it really should be called 'natural.'"

Impressed, the Crone exclaimed, "That's right! And that's where all the confusion arises, isn't it? That's where it all starts because most people tend to associate magic with so many kinds of supernatural happenings."

"But they're really not supernatural, they're natural happenings."

"Yes," the old woman winked. "I think you discovered that a bit ago when you found out you couldn't come up with an example of true magic, eh?"

"Uh-huh. I first thought about how magical you appeared to look with your hair floating out in the twilight. You know, when we were outside and then . . ."

" . . . then you realized you were comparing that visual to fairytale illustrations found in children's books," finished the Grandmother.

"Yes, found there and a lot of other places, too. Every image I see of a mystical elder being looks just like you did out there."

"Don't you think that the words like 'magical' and 'mystical' automatically come with certain types of associative visuals? Maybe surreal types?"

"Of course."

"And why is that, do you think?"

"Because that's how people want them to look."

"Why?"

"Because that's the visual they want to believe in."

"Mmmm."

"Right?"

"Oh, yes, yes. I didn't mean to imply otherwise, Child.

That's precisely the reason for it. Yet . . . why do you think that is?"

"I guess because people just plain like the whole idea of supernatural things like ghosts, goblins, and elves."

"But ghosts are not supernatural. And fairies aren't either. What about this twilight time meeting we've managed to manifest? Is that a supernatural event? How would you categorize it?"

Little Self had to hesitate a moment before responding. She grinned up at the wise Granny she'd come to deeply love through this physical knowing. "I think it's fun calling it magical, but I know it's not. Not really," she underscored.

"You're right. It's not really magic, eh? Not at all. It's all very natural. Though you and I couldn't sit down together and draw a schematic of this meeting's technicalities, that doesn't matter because, intellectually, we still know and understand that the event itself is completely natural, that it's a matter of physics related to our natural world—to possibilities that have existed all along and long before the human mind's discovery of them."

"Possibilities," the Child pensively whispered. "There's that word again," she sang while toying with the end of her braid that draped over an arm.

"Indeed! There's that word again. And what a loaded word it is too."

"Granny?"

"Mmmm."

"I'm thinking that the terms 'possibilities' and 'magic' could both be used to mean the same thing. Doesn't it seem that way to you?"

"I do, Child. People need to perceive the idea of magic as being undiscovered possibilities existing in their natural world, instead of jumping the gun and calling them supernatural right off the bat."

"Natural possibilities," Little Self said while trying out the sound of the phrase. "So why is the term 'supernatural' even a word then?"

"Ah, doesn't that question circle us right back to where we started?"

"I guess. So . . . so we're right back to the 'why,' aren't we?"

A silvery brow rose. "Depends on which 'why' you're talking about, Dear."

"The 'why' of why people have chosen to ignore the fact that magic is just different parts of their natural world's possibilities, why they choose to hold onto the idea of supernatural things."

"And would you like to hazard a guess for that?"

"Ummm, I think it's because people feel a need for something really, really special to believe in. I think it's because their need is so great that they voluntarily ignore the facts. It's kinda like before, when I said that 'it was fun to think our twilight meeting was some magical event' even though I knew it was really related to natural physics— some little-known rarity of nature—of reality. Even when I already knew that, it was still *fun* to just, well, just *call* it magic."

"Fun," said the elder.

"Yeah, fun. Like most people play with tarot cards because it's fun and others use them as a tool because they really understand them and have a natural skill." The Child's eyes sparkled with mischief. "It was fun seeing you as a magical being before."

"You're a flatterer. Did you know that?"

"It's not flattery. I really did see you like that and it was fun."

"So you think people choose to deny the reality of nature because it's too much fun to call some things magic?"

"Well, I think that's only one reason they do it. I think there must be all kinds of other reasons."

"There are, Little Self. There are all kinds of reasons. Many of those reasons grow from a lack of acceptance of life. When this lack is present in one's life that person will look about for anything they can grasp onto as being uniquely special and, well . . . mystical-sounding.

"Sometimes, through a lack of recognizing one's own specialness of being, people believe they've a need to cast their nets over what they perceive as a supernatural sea of unparalleled uniqueness—magic. That magic, though it be falsely perceived, when brought into their lives, gives them that sense of specialness they thought they felt lacking. Having it makes them feel special."

"But," the Child reasoned, "if magic is only the *natural* possibilities of reality, how can it make anyone feel special?"

"Belief," whispered the Crone. "Belief that it does."

"But then they're just fooling themselves. How can someone truly believe something they know to be false?"

Grandma cleared her throat for sarcastic emphasis "Ahem! Excuse me?"

"What?"

"Ohhh, I think you know the answer to that one. You don't need me to fill in the blanks."

The Child's frown didn't last long before a brightness lighted her face. "The millennium!" she shouted, popping her head up. "When everybody celebrated the wrong date! That was the same thing!"

Silver Hairs nodded.

"It was the exact same thing because people *wanted* to believe in a false fact."

"Yes, Little Self, it was done because it was what people wanted. They had a choice to either align themselves with the facts of reality or to go with what they wanted, yet knew to be false. They chose the falsehood. And, as history bears out, they ended up wanting it so much they became desperate for it to manifest. They wanted themselves right into believing their wants were the reality. That's what desperation does, Little Self. That's a clear, black and white example of what it does to people."

"And also their beliefs," the Child expanded. "For those people reality becomes what they want to believe it to be instead of the other way around."

"That's why reality's nature is often perceived as magic instead of . . ."

The Child finished, "Possibilities."

It wasn't necessary for the old woman to show or verbally express her agreement over the youngster's choice of words. They both knew it was the right one.

"There's still one more thing that bothers me a little," Little Self admitted.

"What's that, Honey?"

"I've watched the Mother write about magic. I mean, she's used the word when she's wanted to associate an event or experience to the sensation of it being something really, really special. I was wondering if people understand her intent when she uses that word."

"The word 'magic'?"

The Child nodded.

"Are you concerned that she might be perpetuating their false belief as to what it really means?"

"Not exactly. Umm, I don't think I know what I mean. I was just wondering if people understood that when she uses the word 'magic' she's referring to the natural possibilities of reality and how incredibly beautiful and emotionally moving they are?"

The Crone reached her hand across the table.

The Child reached back and clasped it.

"Little Self, I wouldn't let that worry you any longer," she softly said. "From this moment on people will know exactly what she means."

"Why? Why from this moment on?"

With a sparkle of magic twinkling from her eye, she whispered, "You'll see. You'll see."

"When?" the Child anxiously whispered back. "When will I see?"

"Soon," came the gentle, yet cryptically definitive reply, "very soon."

Chapter Twenty-Four

Little Self stood, picked up the rolling pin and resumed working on her project. As the cuckoo clock chimed she silently counted out the number of chirps from the mechanical bird. She waited for the last note of the Edelweiss song to finish playing before she spoke. "Nine," she muttered.

"Come again?" the Crone asked.

"Nine. It's nine o'clock in the evening."

"So it is," said the old woman as she glanced outside then back to the Child. "Is that relevant to something?"

"I dunno. The light out there is still in twilight but here inside . . . time is still ticking away. It seems that it's nine in the evening already."

"Mmmm, time flies too quickly sometimes."

"But I thought time was being held."

"Twilight is being held, Little Self. Just the twilight. When you leave here, when you pass through the garden gate, the light outside will suddenly return to normal, it'll be dark . . . just like it's supposed to be." The Crone chuckled then. "Well, having never experienced this type of event before, I'm guessing that's how it'll be."

"Nine," the Child whispered to herself.

"Eh?"

"I can't believe it's nine o'clock."

"Believe it, Child. Take reality as it comes."

Little Self glanced outside once again. "It's so magical," she said.

"I thought we'd just been through that."

"But it is, Granny. It is!"

"'Tisn't."

"'Tis," the Child shot back.

"Magic is just nature at work, Child."

"Then this nature is a quirk."

"'Tisn't either. There are no quirks in nature. Nature is as nature does. It's the lack of human understanding that sees it as quirky sometimes. Just because we may not always understand nature's ways doesn't mean those natural ways are quirky. We can't go calling things quirks just because we don't understand their mechanics now, can we? Where's the logic or wisdom in that?" The Crone shook her head. "Goodness gracious, that's like a caveman calling fire magic."

"Well then . . . then all this has a magical feeling to it," the Child corrected.

"That's more like it. You can have a magical feel to something as an emotional or receptive sensory response, but the thing itself is not magical. Just as long as you know the difference."

"I get the difference. I know one from the other," declared the Child as she listened to the clock ticking away the minutes in the background.

Without missing a beat in the conversation, the old woman completely changed the subject by asking, "What do you like to do?"

The youngster had no idea what the question meant. "What do you mean?"

"It occurred to me that we've been talking about so many different things that we've not talked about you at all. I asked what you like to do? You know, what are the things you enjoy in life?"

"Oh, well . . . I can't do anything, not really, because I'm only an aspect of the Mother's consciousness."

"Ohhh, Silly, I know that! Yet you can still take enjoyment from the things the Mother does. I'm asking what those things are."

"I like reading. I love it when she reads. I really love going to the bookstore. I could spend all day long in there. Just the smell of the new ink of the texts and the new bindings is so wonderful to me. And she never forgets to browse through the Children's section, so we can look around for new books to add to my shelf. I think the Mother should work in a bookstore."

That brought an outburst of laughter from the old one. "What!"

Little Self grinned. "Well . . . only if she didn't have all that other work to do."

"Oh. I'm so glad you qualified that. So what else?"

"I love going out in the woods and gathering stuff. I love just sitting out there and listening to all there is to listen to, to see all there is to see. Ummm, let's see," she paused. "When I'm outside in late fall and winter I love the smell of the cabin's woodsmoke that drifts around and through the woods. I love the smell of spruce and pine—it's so fresh and sweet. It smells better than chocolate!" she added.

Though this last was said in complete innocence and not intended as a joke, the Crone found it hilariously amusing. She laughed.

Little Self frowned. "Why are you laughing at me?"

"Oh, Honey, you're a treasure. I'm not laughing at you, I'm just so tickled by your honest spontaneity. It tickles this old woman's heart to see it so freely expressed. It makes my heart laugh."

The Child didn't handle compliments well. She blushed. "Oh." Then, in an effort to quickly extract herself from the embarrassing situation, she began to ramble. "I love the crackle and snap of the fire in the woodstove when we're sitting around the living room at night with just candles burning, I love candlelight. . . . I love the smell of the incense we burn because it smells like the woods . . . also I love watching the deer when they hang around the house, especially when they lie down by the birdbath and . . ."

"Little Self!"

"What! What!" the Child snapped back, unable to put on the brakes quick enough to stop her speeding runaway barrage of words.

"Are you running some kind of verbal marathon or something? Slow down! You're making me dizzy!"

"I am?"

The Crone made a point of wiping her brow. "Whew, Child. You can jabber faster than a crow scolding a hawk!"

The Child liked the visual she got of that. "I can?" she beamed. "Crows can get squawking pretty fast."

"Not as fast as you, Little Self. You got them beat by a country mile."

The little one's grin widened. "A country mile," she repeated. "I like the sound of that. That's another thing I like. I like certain word phrases that are colorful and bring comforting visuals to the mind. What about you, Granny? What do you like?"

"Ohhh, same as you, Little Self. Same as you."

The Child squinted suspiciously at the elder. "Talk about slick."

"Slick? I'm too old to get slick. I wasn't trying to avoid your question, I was just answering it. I do like the same things as you. I could add gardening but what would that do when you love it too and just forgot to include it?"

"I also forgot to include puppies."

"Now look who's getting slick, you little imp."

The Child flashed a dramatized look of innocence. "How is saying that I love puppies being slick?"

"Oh, no-no-no," the old woman admonished while wagging her finger at the girl. "No, you don't. You don't go pulling that play-acting on me."

Little Self giggled.

The elder grinned.

"Still," the Child had the nerve to say, "I still love puppies."

And the Crone, well, the Crone just sighed.

Chapter Twenty-Five

It took another forty-five minutes for the two to finish up their jobs of grinding eggshells and bones into powder and mixing them together. Once the blend was emptied into new containers they worked to clean up the leftover mess and put their tools away.

As the last drawer and cupboard was being closed, Little Self heard a sound from outside. "What's that?"

"What's what?"

"That noise. That rumbling sound."

The old woman tilted her head to listen. "Sounds to me like a truck with a bad muffler."

Little Self's eyes widened to the size of full moons. "Sally!" she squealed, rushing to the back door and flying down the steps. "It's Sally!" she shouted.

The screen door slammed shut with a bang behind the Child.

Grandma let her eyes scan the room. They rested on the new sage bundles hanging about. She sighed. And turned toward the door.

Reluctantly the Crone made her way down the steps. In her hand was the Child's basket cradling Raggedy Ann. The old woman's heart was beating like a thousand drums thundering in the night, for she knew that Sally's appearance was the one sign that marked the end to the twilight meeting. Now it was her time to wear a mask. The mask had a broad smile. "Well, I'll be!" she exclaimed. "It is Sally!"

Hanging arms over the top of the gate, Little Self was shaking with excitement as she watched the pickup slow to a stop and saw Granny's long-time friend climb down from the seat.

"Little Self!" Sally cried out. "What a surprise to see you here!"

The Child giggled. "Hi, Sally! I've been here for a long time. We had great fun!"

"Good! Good! I'm glad to hear that," she replied while reaching over the bench seat to gather up her gardening supplies.

Little Self was so excited she hopped from one foot to the other. Impatiently she waited for Sally to close the distance between the vehicle and the gate.

Seeing how loaded down Sally was, the Child unlatched the gate and swung it wide. She was mindful not to take a step beyond the flagstone pathway. "You have an armful!" she chirped.

Once inside the gate, Sally leaned down to kiss the Child's cheek.

Little Self immediately wrapped her arms around the other's neck and held tight. "I love you, Sally. Thank you for taking care of Granny all these years."

"No need to thank me, Little Self, but you're welcome just the same." Then Sally winked and whispered, "I have a secret in here," she said, indicating the picnic basket in her hand. "Wait till you see!"

The Child didn't need to wait for she could hear whimpering sounds coming from inside. Her hand quickly covered her grinning mouth as Granny came up to them.

The old woman, noticing the new picnic basket, exclaimed, "That's a nice basket someone left us. I could use something like that to hold the pinecones I collect." She then glanced down at Little Self and explained, "Visitors to the abbey leave us things once in a while. Most of the time they're little gifts of food goodies. Once someone left us two fifty-pound bags of sunflower seeds for our birds. We just never know what Sally will find when she goes up there to groom the place." Granny looked down at the Child. "Isn't that nice, Honey? Isn't it nice that people do things like that? Especially when they don't have to?" The old woman sighed. "Nooo, we sure never expected anything like that. People can be so nice, so thoughtful." She then shook her head at the Child. "People don't have to do that, they don't need to leave a thing."

"But they want to, Granny. They want to give a little back to you and Sally for all you've done for them. It's not only for the both of you, it's also for them, too. It makes them feel good inside to do it."

"Well . . . I suppose you're right," the Crone said as she reached out to help with Sally's load. "Here," she said, "let me take those rakes and spades."

Sally nonchalantly turned to expose the basket. "I got those, you take the basket."

Reaching for the wicker handle, the old one felt it tremble in her hands. "My goodness! What's in this?"

Little Self could not hold back her giggling.

Granny looked down at the excited Child then up to her friend's smiling eyes. "Nooo," she crooned as the basket wiggled about. "Don't tell me."

Little Self danced about. "Look inside, Granny. Look inside!"

The old woman looked from one eager set of eyes to the other.

"Granny!" squealed the impatient Child. "Look inside!"

Raising the basket up to her bodice and bending her head close, the Crone lifted one side of the woven lid and peered within. Her breath caught. "Ohhhh," was all she could manage to voice.

The Child was beside herself as she pranced around in ecstatic glee. "Told you so, Granny. I told you so," she sang.

Setting the basket down on the flagstones, the old woman knelt. She lifted out two fluffy, six-week-old Yorkies with pink satin bows tied around their necks. The old woman brought them up to her cheeks and rubbed her face in the soft fur.

The pups whimpered and vigorously covered the salty wet cheek with kisses.

"Oh, you dear, sweet little things!" Granny whispered while rubbing her cheek in the soft, new fur. "Do you not have a home?"

The Child stopped prancing about. "What? Of course they have a home! They *are* home!"

The old woman looked to Sally.

Sally was grinning from ear to ear.

The Crone shifted her gaze to the Child.

Little Self was flashing a Cheshire cat smile.

"Here?" the old woman whispered.

The Child rolled her eyes. "Of course, here. Someone left a special gift for you two, Granny. Somebody wanted you to have puppies to love! See? There's a card attached to the basket. It says: *'To Mary and Sally—Please accept my gift of appreciation for all you've done for me. I couldn't think of a better gift than one that would keep on giving you both continued comfort and love. No gift does that better than a puppy. Love, a grateful friend.'"*

Looking back at the tiny balls of warmth in her hands, the old one began to cry. She cried and cried.

Sally dropped her tools.

Little Self ran forward.

Together they knelt beside the Crone and wrapped their arms about her as she haltingly spoke between sobs. "But I . . . don't want to have to . . . leave them," she cried. "I don't want them to . . . ever have to live . . . missing me. Oh, God . . . I couldn't hurt them like that."

"Look how much they like you," Little Self encouraged the old one to notice.

"We could use a little puppy mischief around the house," Sally added.

"But . . . " the Crone sniffed.

Little Self kept up the pressure. "But they're homeless! Look how helpless they are!"

Sally slathered on the honey. "They've been with me all afternoon. During my gardening breaks we played together and I fed them my lunch. When I rested in the sun they curled up and slept in my lap like babies. I think they've already imprinted our cedar incense smell from my clothes."

Granny looked up. "You think?"

Sally noticed Little Self's worried face as she answered. "I really do think they've already done some imprinting. Somebody left them for us. They knew we'd find them and take 'em home. That person wanted these little pups to have a good, loving home. That person wanted, more than anything, for us and these pups to be together."

"Ohhh," the Crone soothed while caressing the tiny faces. "You're home now, little ones. No more baskets for you. From now on you're going to have an old woman to snuggle up against on cold snowy nights."

"Yippee!" shouted Little Self as she skipped around the flagstones acting like a cheerleader. "Granny's got puppies! Granny's got puppies!"

Wiping her eyes, the old one smiled. "I'm such a mess. Why do these little critters always make me cry so?"

Sally laughed and teasingly tousled the Crone's hair. "Because you're such a sensitive old slob, that's why. Everything makes you cry."

"Nuh-uh," Little Self piped up. "It's because she feels magic!"

Sally frowned with the private joke. "Magic?"

"Yes! Magic! Huh, Granny."

Rubbing the soft down against her cheek, the old woman smiled. "Oh, yes. Pure magic."

The three moved to sit on the porch steps for a time and passed the pups between them, each taking time to pet and fawn over the new additions to the family.

After Little Self excitedly told Sally all about their wonderful day together and how much fun it'd been working on projects and talking about all sorts of things, a peculiar hush fell over the trio.

The Child wanted to ignore it. "Granny?"

"Yes, Child, it's time."

Silence.

Sally turned to hug the little girl. "It was so much fun finally meeting you, Little Self. You're just like I pictured you'd be." She smoothed both of her hands down the long braids. "Now you be a good girl and try not to pop out on the Mother when other people are around, all right?"

Little Self made a face. "I already promised Granny that."

"Okay," Sally smiled, "give me a big hug, then. I've got to get these tools away before the light fades."

They hugged. They hugged for a long while.

Then, as Sally went about her chore, Little Self turned to the Crone who was still holding both pups. "Guess I gotta go now," she whispered.

Granny carefully set the puppies back on the blanket inside the picnic basket and closed the double lids. Trying to conceal the growing lump in her throat, she stood and reached for the Child's basket. "You don't want to forget these," she said.

Little Self reluctantly reached out and wrapped her small fingers around the basket handle. She lifted the doll out and clutched it tightly to her chest. Desperately holding back tears, she softly said, "I'm . . . going to miss you, Granny."

The old woman bent down to wrap her arms around the small girl. "We'll still be together, Honey. In the Mother's consciousness we're always there . . . together. Always."

"I know, but it's not the same as this was."

"No, it's not the same, yet it's still being together. Neither one of us is going anywhere, not really." She tenderly lifted the Child's chin. "We're always together, Honey. We're always together."

Striving to make Granny proud, Little Self took a deep, halting breath and bravely smiled. "I gotta go now. I love you, Granny," she said, placing her hand on the gate latch.

"I know. But first I want you to remember that everything you saw here was . . ."

"Possibility," finished the Child as she longingly gazed back at the cottage. "All of it means possibilities that may happen."

"Yes. And also everything I told you about the abbey, the little green an' gold craft shop, the level of damage from the Changes that brought about the stonework on the place, and . . . and Sally and I still being here in 2040."

Little Self looked down at her scuffed shoes and studied them before returning her gaze to Granny's eyes. "I know. Everything is the result of completed probabilities. I understand that all these things could change at any time. I understand, Granny."

The Crone sweetly smiled and bent down to kiss the top of the Child's head. "Okay then, Honey," she said placing her hand on the gate. "Let's cross this last threshold together then."

They both swung the gate open and passed through the opening.

They let it slam shut behind them.

Standing outside now, Little Self slowly inched away from her beloved Granny. She checked the sky for any change in the light. "Guess we shouldn't try to prolong this," she bravely said.

"Guess not," came the choked reply.

The Child turned.

The Crone swiftly wiped away a tear.

Again Little Self turned and started walking backward. She waved as she moved further away. "Bye, Granny," she said before turning her back to the cottage.

Granny raised her hand. "Bye, Little Self." And she stood watching the precocious little fairy child make her way up the drive.

But then, suddenly, remembering the big secret she needed to share, the Crone quickly called out, "Little Self!"

The Child spun around. "What?"

"Remember. Everything you've seen here and heard about the future are all just probabilities!"

"I'll remember," the Child called back.

The light was beginning to fade.

"Oh, and Little Self!"

"What?"

"Remember about those probabilities?"

"Yes. What about them?" the Child quickly asked while noticing the oncoming darkness.

"You don't need to remember anything about our meeting!"

The old woman's voice was dimming.

"What?" the Child yelled back.

"You don't need to remember anything about our meeting here today!"

"WHY NOT?" Little Self shouted through the thickening atmosphere.

"Because of those PROBABILITIES . . . the Mother managed to JOIN US AFTER ALL!" she hollered. "She was WITH US THE WHOLE TIME! She WROTE DOWN EVERY SINGLE WORD WE SAID!"

Little Self jumped in the air with a big whoop. "YES!" she shouted at the top of her lungs. She immediately hollered back. "Then it's ALL IN THE BOOK?"

"WHAT?" the old woman asked as darkness began settling over her shoulders like a cloak.

"IT'S ALL IN THE BOOK!" the girl repeated like a distant echo.

Little Self just had time enough to see the old woman make a joyful jump in the air over knowing she'd successfully conveyed the secret. "YES!" she'd heard the Crone shout. "YES!"

With a giggle over Granny's antics, the Child turned a final time, her image fading like a morning mist touched by the first warming rays of dawn.

Down by the gate, the Crone regretted not having the time to tell Little Self that the secret was the very reason why the Mother changed the title of the book to *Trined in Twilight*. Then, in remembrance, a warm smile of amusement crept up the corners of her mouth when she recalled what a smartypants Little Self was—she'd figure it all out for herself. Eventually.

Somewhere deep in the dark forest surrounding the old woman's cottage three sounds were heard.

A coyote howled.

A nighthawk called as it sliced through the silvered moonlit valley.

And the last sound, one much quieter, was that of a vanishing garden gate, opening . . . then closing.